DOING
BUSINESS
IN THE
EUROPEAN
UNION

DOING
BUSINESS
IN THE
EUROPEAN
UNION

THIRD EDITION

Paul Gibbs

KOGAN
PAGE

First published in 1990
Second edition published in 1992
Third edition published in 1994

Kogan Page Limited
120 Pentonville Road
London N1 9JN

© Paul Gibbs, 1990, 1992, 1994

British Library Cataloguing in Publication Data
A CIP record for this book is available from the British Library.

ISBN 0 7494 1323 9

Typeset by BookEns Ltd, Baldock, Herts
Printed in England by Clays Ltd, St Ives plc

CONTENTS

LIST OF FIGURES

LIST OF TABLES

PREFACE TO THE FIRST EDITION

Many books giving information on the European Community exist for businesspeople but few, if any, address the issue of personal interaction with foreign clients in a foreign culture, in the pursuit of business abroad. A potential market of 320 million consumers will, of course, have attractions for all nations. Having a good product or service with good promotion might be sufficient in your home market, but in the European Community many more companies can, and will, claim the same advantages. The choice of business partner will more often than not depend on personal rapport. This book is about creating the right impression, making sure you have a valuable insight into each country's business culture, its behavioural patterns and consumer trends. It will ensure that you do not let avoidable circumstances obstruct your business potential.

Each chapter deals with the process of making and retaining a business contact abroad. The book highlights changes in culture and etiquette, and looks at the different spending habits of consumers throughout the European Community. It also briefly examines the corporate structures of each country's organisations, as well as how to address senior staff, and provides handy tips on conforming to standards of dress.

Being aware of each other's customs and taking the time to prepare yourself for your client's benefit rather than your own will not make a bad product good, nor a good product better, but it will help a good product to be accepted, thus increasing sales and profitability.

PREFACE TO THE SECOND EDITION

The second edition of this book adds a commentary on the success of the Maastricht European Council, which paves the way to both monetary and political union. Although union with whom is a difficult question to answer! The Community has attracted eager advances from both East and West. The creation of a new European Economic Area (EEA) with the countries of the European Free Trade Association (EFTA) has expanded the Single Market to over 380 million consumers. The inclusion of Austria, Finland, Iceland, Liechtenstein, Norway, Sweden and Switzerland into the free-trade environment for goods, services, capital and people was the natural expansion as EFTA was both the EC's largest export market and most important supplier. The 19 countries of the EEA will also co-ordinate social, educational, environmental and other policies, excluding the common agricultural policy. The EEA is meant to represent the benefits of full membership of the EC while restricting political power to shape the EEA to full EC members. In this way, the commitment given by EFTA members to seek full membership of the Community retains some additional value to them.

The East has been no less enthusiastic for a new European order. The collapse of the Council of Mutual Economic Assistance (CMEA) led three ex-Soviet bloc countries – Czechoslovakia, Hungary and Poland – to apply for, and receive, Associate Membership of the EC. These countries are looking for full economic as well as political union with the rest of Europe.

The rate of change is accelerating. It seems inconceivable that by the beginning of the second millennium the European Community will resemble anything like that envisaged by the original signatories to the Treaty of Rome. The extent of change in Eastern Europe, the unification of Germany, EEA and the difficulties being faced in the GATT negotiations certainly mean that we suffer the fate of living in 'interesting times'.

I hope the inclusion of the new chapter (Chapter 7), dealing with Eastern and Central Europe, widens the usefulness of the book.

Paul Gibbs

PREFACE TO THE THIRD EDITION

1993 has passed and the community is now a union operating within the Maastricht Treaty. Many of the free trade directives have been enacted by sovereign governments within a world economic climate which has been liberated following the successful GATT agreement, but is also reflective of huge free trading areas. The tension between NAFTA and the Japanese and Pacific Rim trading blocs forces European businessmen to look outside Europe to defend their markets. In fact, the future for Europe after the single market provisions is global.

The strengthening, for that is what it is, of both the political determination of the Union and its widening influence on Eastern bloc countries is likely to continue. It is difficult to predict the political desire for a fully integrated Union, following the failure of the EMS and the bumpy road of European foreign policy. However, the generation of new consumers educated in European business schools now probably have more in common with their European colleagues than with their national peers. It is with them, the multi-lingual, flexible, non-nationalistically bound Europeans, that the future of the Union depends. The level playing fields introduced within the single market make a harmonious trading area possible, but significant attitude changes are required to make it an integrated whole.

This book acts both as a core reference to European activities and as a country-by-country business guide. Kogan Page publish a range of useful additional texts which the reader may find of value. I would recommend the following:

Selling to Europe, Roger Bennett
1993 amd Beyond, James Dudley
European Marketing, Richard Lynch
European Community Funding for Business Development, Rona Michie and Kevin Allen
Europe 2002, Bengt Wahlstrom

ACKNOWLEDGEMENTS

Many people have helped provide information for this book —
from trade associations, embassies, financial institutions
(especially Touche Ross) and other authorities. I thank them
all. In particular, I thank Jane Holliday for her research, editing,
typing and enthusiasm.

I thank Ben & Simon because I want to.

PART I
PREPARING FOR SUCCESS IN THE SINGLE EUROPEAN MARKET

INTRODUCTION

Europe is the biggest potential free market to open this century. But, in a sense, it has never been closed. True, national culture, customs and patriotism have constituted both tariff and non-tariff barriers, but very few countries have operated a total boycott which could not in some way have been overcome, given the will. (The Dutch and the Luxembourgers in fact achieved it long before 1992.) However, the unified European market without trade barriers, which was realised during 1993, presents an opportunity for co-operation and competition on an equal footing between countries which has not previously existed. The harmonisation programme has produced a framework more suitable for pan-European initiative, increased efficiency and lower prices, that applies to the few, but growing, (both large and small) nineteen companies that have prepared themselves well.

Those companies which not only take the time to evaluate the special conditions of other foreign markets, but also take time to study customer preferences and business subcultures will stand the best chance of expanding their businesses and maximising their profits from membership of the European Union.

Much has already been written on consumer preference; the oft-quoted example being the key features of the domestic washing machine which appeal to certain nations (front-loaders for the British, controls on the top for the Germans and spin lock for the Italians), but little has been written on the different ways of doing business. This book attempts to do this.

Britain, and more recently perhaps Denmark, rightly or wrongly, has often been considered the 'odd country out', vetoing rather than agreeing. So before exploring the detail country by country, how does one particular EU member's infrastructure (namely the UK) stand up to examination when compared with other major European Union countries? The conclusion is, unfortunately, not well. In a survey carried out by a leading management accountancy firm, the four European countries geographically nearest to Britain were compared on a range of criteria: location, internationalism, efficiency and reliability. On a ranking system where 1 represents the best and 5 the worst, they scored as follows:

Table A   Five EU countries' infrastructure scoring

| | Number of Scores | |
	Highest	Lowest
Great Britain	4	10
France	11	4
Germany	2	7
Netherlands	15	0
Belgium	4	4

Clearly, Britain has by no means a natural lead in doing business in Europe, nor is there any advantage for countries to choose Britain as the route through which to do such business. Her slowness in providing an infrastructure to link the trans-European high speed rail system is evidence of this.

Table B   Infrastructure ratings of five EU countries

	Ranking	1	2	3	4	5
Location:	airport	NL	GB	D	F	B
	road transport	NL	D	B	F	GB
Local characteristics:						
international:	secondary schooling	B	NL	F	GB	D
	higher education	NL	D	B	F	GB
	mastery of foreign languages	NL	B	D	F	GB
	export quotes of GDP	B	NL	D	GB	F
	direct investment abroad	NL	GB	F	D	B
	product acceptance abroad	NL	D	B	GB	F
efficient:	rental value offices	NL	B	D	F	GB

Ranking	1	2	3	4	5
rental value industrial	NL	B	D	F	GB
building cost offices	B	F	NL	D	GB
building cost industrial	NL	B	F	D	GB
value added per labour unit	F	NL	D	GB	B
wage increases/ common currency	GB	F	NL	B	D
real interest rates	D	F	NL	GB	B
total tele-communications	GB	NL	F	B	D
digital leased circuits	NL	F	B	GB	D
average pay, chief executives	B	NL	GB	F	D
cost of living	NL	B	D	GB	F
corporate tax rates, small companies	GB	B	NL	F	D
corporate tax rates, larger companies	GB	NL	F	B	D
ROI US companies all industries	NL	B	F	D	GB
ROI US companies manufacturing	D	F	NL	B	GB
reliable: stability of a country	NL	D	GB	B	F
way labour affects companies	NL	D	B	F	GB
working days lost in industry	NL	D	F	GB	—

Missing from this list is a country's will to be European. The public announcements by Messrs Heath, Heseltine and Major in support of greater European unity and expansion, contrast sharply with the ex-Prime Minister Thatcher's concern for the growth of a social Europe. Prime Minister Major's true colours are yet to be seen, even after Maastricht, but they seem to be more based in the red, white and blue than in Europe's gold and blue.

To illustrate these issues, the accountants Ernst and Young have recently produced a study which looked at the most attractive locations for a number of industries. Using the example of a motor component supplier, they have constructed a value

Table C Motor Components Supplier

Location Criteria:	West Midlands	East Midlands	North East	Limburg, Belgium	Germany (Bavaria, NRW, Baden Wuerttemberg)	Piedmont, Italy	Alsace	Valencia, Spain	Poland	Hungary
Proximity to market:	5	5	5	5	5	5	5	5	5	5
Grants and incentives:	3	3*	4	3	1	1	3*	3	4*	3
Labour availability:	5	4	5	4	4	4	4	4	4	4
Low production costs:	4	4	4	3	2	3	3	3	5	4

* If located in areas of structural unemployment

5 = Excellent
4 = Good
3 = Moderate
2 = Poor
1 = Does not match the criteria

matrix of sites. These target sites were selected based upon their closeness to existing manufacturers, proximity to new manufacturers and Eastern Europe's government encouragement. As Table C shows clearly, the major threat comes from Eastern Europe! Their integration into the Union when it comes is unlikely to be all plain sailing.

EUROPEAN ELECTIONS

Simultaneous (or almost simultaneous) elections for all member states for membership of the European Parliament have been the norm since 1979. Each country uses its own system which, with the exception of the UK, gives some form of proportional representation. The elections of 15 June 1989 took place in Ireland, Denmark, Spain and the UK (proportional representation in Northern Ireland). The Netherlands, France, Germany, Italy, Belgium, Greece and Luxembourg voted on 18 June 1989.

The electoral systems used for the elections were as follows:

Belgium	Proportional representation by lists. The seats are split 13 for Flemish-speaking areas, 11 for the French- and German-speaking. Voters can cast votes for an entire party list or for individual candidates. Total membership 16. Percentage voting: 1984 92.2 per cent; 1989 90.7 per cent
Denmark	Proportional representation by list. Votes can be cast for an entire party or individual candidates. Total membership 16. Percentage voting: 1984 52.5 per cent; 1989 46.2 per cent
France	Proportional representation by party lists. Each party puts forward a national list of candidates who are elected in proportion to the party's national share at the vote. Parties with less than 5 per cent are excluded. Total membership 81. Percentage voting: 1984 56.7 per cent; 1989 48.7 per cent
Germany	Proportional representation by party lists put forward at national or regional level. Candidates are elected in proportion to the party's share of the vote. Total membership 81.

Greece

Percentage voting: 1984 56.8 per cent; 1989 62.3 per cent
Proportional representation by party list. Total membership 24.

Ireland

Percentage voting: 1984 77.2 per cent; 1989 79.9 per cent
Single transferable votes in four constituencies. Total membership 15.

Italy

Percentage voting: 1984 47.6 per cent; 1989 68.3 per cent
Proportional representation by party lists in five regional constituencies and voters choose both party and individual candidates. Seats are allocated to the parties' share of the votes at regional level. Total membership 81.

Luxembourg

Percentage voting: 1984 83.9 per cent; 1989 81.0 per cent
Proportional representation by lists. Total membership 6.

The Netherlands

Percentage voting: 1984 82 per cent; 1989 87.4 per cent
Proportional representation by lists and seats are allocated by share of the vote at national level. Total membership 25.

Portugal

Percentage voting: 1984 50.5 per cent; 1989 47.2 per cent
Proportional representation by lists. Total membership 24.

Spain

Percentage voting: 1986 72.7 per cent; 1989 51.2 per cent
Proportional representation by lists and seats allocated by share of the vote at national level. Total membership 60.

UK

Percentage voting: 1986 68.9 per cent; 1989 54.8 per cent
Individual elections in 78 single member constituencies in the UK; in Northern Ireland, single transferable vote in a single constituency covering the whole of the country. Three MEPs elected. Total membership 81.

Percentage voting: 1984 UK 32.6 per cent, NI 47.6 per cent; 1989 UK 36.2 per cent, NI 47.7 per cent

The political shape of the Parliament and the mandate it has to take Europe into a new, barrier-free society impacts on business decisions. The most significant trend of the 1989 elections was the move towards a more socialist Parliament and an environmentally-aware electorate. This trend in voting mirrors the trends referred to later in this book under 'Consumer Trends'.

This book does not intend to offer answers to the political and sovereignty issues. Rather, it is addressed to those who are going to do business in the European Union and who may need some help.

The first three chapters deal with the background to the community's development, the essence of international marketing, and pointers to understanding behaviours of a non-verbal character within member states. Then each country is addressed in a fairly consistent manner, although an exact format approach has been avoided in order to allow individual country differences to emerge. (For instance, there is greater emphasis on eating in Spain and rather less in the Netherlands.) The last part of each chapter deals with setting up a business in the country, its management structure, information on letter writing and marketing infrastructure.

Of course, no individual is exactly the same as another, nor can any nation be more than a focused unit of individuals, but gross differences can generally be observed and some of these, where they impact on business transactions, are reported here. Not all apply in all circumstances, but they do give a pointer, at the very least, as to what to expect.

If any overriding business behaviours emerge throughout the book, they may be summarised as:

● Be polite; very polite.
● Be prepared; very prepared.
● Be patient; very − well, enough to trade off time spent and potential reward.

I
INTERNATIONAL MARKETING

The dismantling of psychological and geographical barriers to the purchase of your goods can only be assisted by the harmonisation of the standards, working practices and monetary union within the Single Market. And it can only be achieved with strong international marketing skills which include identifying international marketing opportunities, analysing the chosen geographic market's infrastructure and then deciding upon an entry strategy. Having successfully completed these, it is necessary to assess the impact of international markets upon price, distribution and the logistical problem of manufacture and delivery, the promotion of the product in an international environment and, finally, the centralised or decentralised control of a multinational marketing operation must be faced and resolved.

WHY GO ABROAD?

Generally, the reasons for even considering an international expansion of a company's activities fall into four separate areas:

1. market size (leading to product effectiveness and competitive edge);
2. external influences (economic healthiness or less intense competition than home markets);
3. geographical diversification (in place of product range extension or business diversification); and
4. product longevity (where international sales of a product would make that product's trading cycle more robust).

This seems a very logical approach, but why Europe? It is important to remember that by far the easiest way of promoting business growth is through the expansion of existing markets. In coming to the conclusion that Europe may offer exciting opportunities for your business, do ensure that you are not ignoring the possibilities of your own home market, or those of other major economic trading blocks.

Given that international diversification makes sound sense, and your existing market position is secure, how do you go about selecting the appropriate country? All markets are dynamic and react to their own particular mixture of socio-cultural, political, legal and governmental traits. Understanding the direction and the stability of these 'environments' are just as important, as they either relate to consumer choice or they affect the logistical decisions regarding distribution, manufacturing and promotion.

Awareness of social and cultural norms has helped major multinational companies such as Coca Cola, IBM, Marlboro and Pepsi succeed in being recognised as truly international brands. It also helps the British salespeople to understand the prejudices with which they are met and enables them to overcome them. In a recent study of Swedish, Italian, French and German buyers of heavy engineering products, the following stereotyping of the British emerged:

- low productivity;
- non-competitive pricing strategies;
- poor and unresponsive product design;
- poor marketing.

Certainly this is changing, but it is surprising that Britain has any heavy engineering products at all!

The cultural tapestry of many foreign countries (including Europe) is unavailable to British businesspeople because of language barriers. Little or no mastery of the language leaves an understanding of a country to third-hand interpretation. The tonal shades of the aesthetic qualities of community life are lost and with them the depth of relationship which facilitates serious business transactions.

Economic analysis, however, is generally available from many sources, and enables gross and objective evaluation of a market's potential. Of critical importance in any review are the trading practices of the country or countries concerned. Although General Agreement on Tariffs and Trade (GATT) has done much to reduce tariff barriers throughout the world, it has not done (and nor could it do) much to reduce the importance of non-tariff barriers such as chauvinism (eg the Australian 'buy Australian and be proud' campaign).

Table 1.1   Percentage of adults speaking European languages

	Belg	Den	Fra	Ger	Ire	It	Neth	Sp	UK
	%	%	%	%	%	%	%	%	%
English	26	51	26	43	99	13	68	13	100
French	71	5	100	18	12	27	31	15	15
German	22	48	11	100	2	6	67	3	6
Italian	4	1	8	3	1	100	2	4	1
Spanish	3	1	13	1	1	5	4	100	2
Flemish/Dutch	68	1	1	3	–	–	100	–	1

Note No figures available for Portugal, Greece or Luxembourg.
Source G/AA

Headway has been made towards the goal of a free market, but in reality the EU itself is not without its own hypocritical interpretations. The EU has particular anti-dumping measures regarding steel, textiles and heavy engineering equipment. But as the steel industry has experienced, what is at one time legitimate business practice, can become unacceptable protectionism leading to 'excessive' profits within five short years. The French have their own way of dealing with the problem, whether it be British lamb or Japanese video cassettes. The French psyche can construct such complications that it becomes impossible actively to develop the market.

Political risk is also a key area of the evaluation. Although the EU does not suffer the extravagant and violent swings of fundamentalist Moslem states or the overt corruption of Latin America, nevertheless, the damage caused by changing personal tax rates, politically-driven currency valuations or nationalisation policies can ruin business plans designed upon a stable political environment. The tragedy of the once-prosperous Yugoslavia is a case in point. But things are changing both inside member states and in the outside communities looking in. In Amsterdam, for instance, by the year 2000 more children will be born with non-Dutch parents than with Dutch. Most of these are expected to be followers of Islam. Social integration of differing ethnic non-European traditions, must be a high priority for all of Europe if political and social unrest are to be avoided. For a more detailed discussion of Europe beyond the year 2000, I suggest the book *Europe 2002: Looking Ahead to a New Europe* by Bengt Wahlstrom, published by Kogan Page. A political risk assessment technique has been developed at the University of

Delaware. It ranks each selected country on 15 economic, political and financial factors and gives the country a rating between zero and one hundred.

Finally, consumer data. Although standardisation has become more common, a universal quantitative measure which can give meaningful pan-European relative comparisons has not yet been found. Measurements such as the percentage of the population with a university education may give some insight, but many indirect UK measurements are so open to distortion that they become no more than broad brush pointers when applied to many European countries. To test consumer reaction to any product proposition requires a local visit.

However, before such a visit, much information can be collected from the Department of Trade and Industry, the British Overseas Trade Board, the Commission of the European Communities, the European Investment Bank, the United Nations Commission for Europe, banks, investment houses, trade associations and Chambers of Commerce.

Having undertaken a wide-ranging international study (grants are available from the DTI) and having made a decision on the appropriateness of a marketing venture, the entry strategy has to be considered. In essence, there are five ways in which products can be sold to foreign consumers:

1. Through agents (UK embassies and foreign trade associations can help in selection).
2. Through external distributors (sole distributors of products acting as principals).
3. Through external management control on indigenous enterprises (for example, Hilton Hotels).
4. Through franchising (for example, Benetton).
5. Through licensing (for example, Mickey Mouse).

Each of these has specific advantages and weaknesses and suits distinct types of business at different states of their international marketing development. Table 1.2 highlights the cost of entry with the expected climate for new international ventures.

It is obvious, therefore, that highly-committed companies are likely to receive the best host support, because not only do they create economic wealth within the country directly related to the product but also through companies servicing them. But the cost is high and so is the risk. To balance that, the managment product-to-sales chain is more under control, marketing knowledge is more extensive and appropriate long-term

Table 1.2 Entry strategy guide

WELCOMING INVESTMENT CLIMATE

		HIGH	MEDIUM	LOW
C O S T O F E N T R Y	HIGH	Wholly owned joint venture	Assemby	Franchising
	MEDIUM	Joint equity venture	Industrial co-operation	Know-how, contracts
	LOW	Sales	Management contracts	Exporting

Source Stanley J Paliwoda, *International Marketing*

objectives more realisable. Certainly, the cost of exporting to a country and using agents would seem, on the surface, a lower risk, but with little or no actual control over the promotion of your product, spurious management information can be generated, which makes expansion decisions very much harder.

It is unlikely that the product being offered exactly matches the new market's needs, although this should be less of a European Union problem post-1992. The product policy decisions themselves fall into two groups: product modification and standardisation. McDonald's, 7-Up, Benetton, Disney World, International Traveller hotels and 'high net worth' banking have all taken the route of seeking product economies of scale and reduction in development costs. Larger budgets, uncomplicated products and actual market segmentation can create receptive markets.

Other product categories may not be so lucky. Modifications can be necessitated by legal requirements, tariffs, nationalism, technical requirements, taxation, climate and, of course, consumer tastes.

The costs of matching these manifest and hidden restrictions need to be understood and incorporated into the pricing of the product. Alcoholic drinks tailor both their strength and image to fit local markets. Obvious pricing elements contribute to the competitive edge of the product, such as local worker pay rates, accommodation, exchange controls, currency invoicing and other export overheads. Each of these will influence which cell in the entry strategy guide should be used.

THE PROMOTION OF GLOBAL PRODUCTS

There are few, if any, truly global products that take on a 'personality' or status which enhances the consumer's use or consumption, for which (usually) he is prepared to pay a premium. The top brands in the largest European countries tend to reflect the national personalities. In France, the strongest brands include Cointreau, Moet & Chandon, Chanel No 5 and Yves St. Laurent; in Germany, Der Spiegel, Mercedes-Benz and Melitta; in Italy, Ferrari, Fiat and Martini; and in the more conservative UK, the BBC, Kit-Kat and Marks and Spencer. In the world economy the major brands are dominated by American companies. These are, in order of leadership; Coca-Cola, Kellogg's, McDonald's, Kodak, Marlboro, IBM, American Express, Sony, Mercedes and Nescafe.

Only sound investigation into all of the many elements of an international promotion campaign will give it the best chance of success. Public relations, packaging, sales promotion, advertising and direct response must all be carefully considered. For instance, direct response may seem a good idea, but what about postal regulations, currency instability? And how about the product name? Will it travel? Take the examples of SIC and PSCHITT (two French soft drinks), BUM (a Spanish potato chip) and SUPER PISS (a Finnish product for unfreezing car door locks). Less obvious is the pronunciation factor; for example, the pronunciation of Park Lane cigarettes causes difficulties for speakers of the Spanish language, thus sales are bound to be slow. And finally, translation. It is not just the accuracy of the translation which is critical but also the underlying concepts, thoughts and ideas that are conveyed within the translation. Below are some absurdities created by literal translation:

Table 1.3 Translation absurdities

Message in English	Translated Meaning
Come alive with Pepsi	Rise from the grave (Germany)
Schweppes Tonic Water	Schweppes bathroom water (Italy)
Chrysler for power	Chrysler is an aphrodisiac (Spain)

USEFUL ADDRESSES

The European Union LINGUA programme aims to promote a quantitative and qualitative improvement in foreign language competence in order to develop communication skills within the workforce.

UK LINGUA Unit
Seymour Mews House
Seymour Mews
London W1H 9PE
Tel: 071-224 1477
Fax: 071-224 1906

Belfast LINGUA Office
Central Bureau Office
16 Malone Road
Belfast BT9 5BW
Tel: 0232 664418

Edinburgh LINGUA Office
Central Bureau Office
3 Bruntsfield Crescent
Edinburgh EH1 04HD
Tel: 031 447 8024

2
THE EUROPEAN UNION – THE STORY SO FAR

By 1992, the 12 countries of the European Community had a free trade union which, in theory, should have enhanced the economic and social lives of over 320 million people that make up its population. This economic power, a GDP greater than the USA and over 250 per cent of the world average, and about one-third of the world's exports, should position it as the third major player in world affairs alongside the USA and Japan (rapidly growing in political as well as economic influence). However,the results of the past 10 years show only declining overseas trade, high production costs and lower investment in research and development. The challenge remains, and a unified Europe which has grown in internal strength is yet to match its global competitors.

Unity, however, requires goodwill on behalf of the Union's national governments, as well as a change in the cultural perceptions of the individual countries. Andrew Shonfield, in a BBC Reith Lecture in 1972, described the Community thus:

'It is more like a bag of marbles than a melting-pot, the marbles are soft on the surface and made of some sticky substance, like putty, which keeps them clinging together as they are pushed around and constantly make contact with one another in the bag. It does not sound very attractive; it certainly is not very coherent. It is much less satisfactory to describe than the simplified version of a supranational European government which was the ideal of the founding fathers of the community.'

Be that as it may, the European Union has enlarged itself and dealt with some of the urgent problems created by the Common

Agricultural Policy. The UK, a member since 1 January 1973, has found, and continues to find, its European feet and identity. France, it seems, is suspicious of UK intentions but full of self-importance (as was shown in the recent GATT negotiations over status) as a founder member.

New members are fighting for domestic recognition and not European best advantage. The enlargement debate continues, directly affecting EFTA members. More difficult discussions will concern not the hapless central European countries embracing communism, but the low cost, high technology economies into which they will develop. Already many in Europe look to these geographical neighbours as the main source not of new markets but of competitors.

HISTORICAL BACKGROUND

The growth of a European federation is certainly not a new idea, even given its modern-day stimulus from the atrocities of the Second World War and a desire to keep the peace between France and West Germany. As early as the fourteenth century, Pierre Dubois proposed a European Confederation to be governed by a European Council. Britain's own William Penn in 1693 suggested a European Parliament as a means of securing a peaceful Europe. But it was the close of the Second World War and the ensuing economic, defensive and political needs that were the catalysts which led to the signing by six countries – France, West Germany, Italy, the Netherlands, Belgium and Luxembourg – of the Treaty of Rome on 25 March 1957 and the creation of the EEC on 1 January 1958.

The original agreement committed the six countries to a far-reaching exercise of economic integration over a 12-year period. Between 1958 and 1969, the 'six' created the kind of economic community envisaged in the Rome treaty. The basic elements of customs union, internal tariff and quota dismantlement, and the construction of the common external tariff were established ahead of schedule. Non-tariff barriers were attacked, the Common Agricultural Policy was operational and trade and arrangements with colonial dependencies were devised.

Britain had participated in early discussions but, for many reasons, joined Norway, Sweden, Denmark, Austria, Switzerland and Portugal in establishing the European Free Trade Association. She quickly recognised, however, that the EEC was the route most likely to fulfil her aims.

Thus in 1961 Britain applied for full membership of the EEC. Negotiations were, however, abruptly terminated in 1963, as were the applications for fellow EFTA countries Norway and Denmark, and a separate application by the Republic of Ireland. New negotiations began in 1969 which ultimately led, through a more committed and sensitive approach by the British Government, to membership on 1 January 1973. All four nations were accepted, but Norway, after a national referendum, declined membership. Britain renegotiated its terms in 1975 and, having put these to a national referendum, gained overwhelming support to retain its membership.

The second enlargement of the Community came with the membership of Greece and the Iberian countries of Spain and Portugal. Trading ties between these countries and the Community were in place long before their full membership of the Community. The turning point seemed to be the return of democracy in these countries. Their election to membership in all but political terms weakened the union, increased the population base by one-fifth and the GNP by one-tenth. Membership came first to Greece on 1 January 1981, and then to Portugal and Spain on 1 January 1986. All three have underdeveloped economies and have been given an extended period to conform with the directives of the Community.

The most significant event on the road to securing European union since the Treaty of Rome is the Single European Act. In 1985 the heads of state agreed to a programme comprising 300 separate pieces of legislation. To facilitate the enactment of these, the Luxembourg Summit of 1985 adopted several proposals prepared to create a European union and then, in February 1986, the Single European Act. The Act replaces the unanimity required for any enactment of Community legislation. It permits decisions to be made by a qualifying majority of ministers with regard to measures which have the establishing and functioning of the internal market as their principal objective.

The Act covers a broad spectrum and such diverse areas as economic and social cohesion, environment, co-operation between institutions, and political co-operation. The adoption of the Act stopped the practice of travelling at the pace of the slowest dissenting member and showed a political will to dispense with the inefficiencies of fragmentation and so provides a unified market.

The most important European event since the Single European Act was the Heads of States or Governments meeting held in Maastricht on 9–10 December, 1991. The chief results of the summit were the agreement between those present on a draft Treaty on European Union, which is due for ratification on 1 January, 1993. In particular, it signalled the launch of a gradual but irreversible process towards economic, social and monetary union (although the UK and Denmark were granted exemptions).

The provision of a common forum and security policy has been tested by the events in the former Yugoslavia and has responded well, given the political reality of the event. Economic union has taken a considerable set-back due to international currency speculation in EMS currencies. The economic justification for a single currency remains strong, but what the central bankers need to do is to find a method to protect sovereign currencies in the convergence process. This will not, however, deal with the psychological machismo exhibited by some nations to see the symbol of their independence on their own currency. In a more liberal and enlarged Union this should be more possible, particularly if voting procedures are amended. However, it is unlikely that this will occur by the initial target date of 1999.

The European Council also decided on a protocol for 11 of the 12 member states (the UK being the dissenting member), the purpose of which is adopting and implementing the Charter of the Fundamental Social Rights of Workers. Also, there were advances on the basis of co-operation in the spheres of justice and home affairs. Food was pledged to the emerging Commonwealth of Independent States and their process of democratisation was welcomed.

One aspect of the conference which did not receive wide publicity was the declaration on racism and xenophobia. Quoting directly from the Bulletin of the European Community Commission, 'the European Council expresses its conviction that respect for human dignity is essential to the Europe of the Community, and that combatting discrimination in all its forms is therefore vital to membership of that Community'. These sentiments apply equally to existing as well as potential members, and particular reference was made to the nationalism manifesting itself throughout Eastern Europe.

The Maastricht agreement was claimed to represent a good deal for UK business, as Peter Lilley, the then Secretary of State for Trade and Industry, put it: 'First, we remain free to tailor our employment and social policies to our own needs. Second, we have reaffirmed the country's commitment to open markets and free competition. Thirdly, we have put the potentially damaging industry text under lock and key.'

Enlargement is the next issue for the Union. Four nations; Finland, Austria, Norway and Sweden, have all gained provisional membership. They bring 26 million new consumers to add to the 345 million currently in the Union, and have already accepted most of the body of community law through their previous negotiations for membership of the European economic area. Domestic decisions will still need to be confirmed but, as the table below shows, they can look forward to growth in their GNP to match that of other Union members. The Union itself benefits from the inclusion of net contributors and prosperous markets.

Table 2.1 Comparative GNP

	1986	1992	% Growth
USA	4128.33	4623.5	12
Japan	1378.55	1763.8	28
Austria*	65.95	79.2	20
Belgium	81	95.6	18
Denmark	60.16	64.1	6
Finland*	55.18	57.8	5
France	535.07	620.5	16
Germany	633.08	761.8	20
Greece	33.98	37.5	10
Ireland	18.73	25.1	34
Italy	436.91	505.2	15
Luxembourg	3.62	4.6	27
Netherlands	131.58	153.6	17
Norway*	60.61	66	8
Portugal	21.54	26.8	24
Spain	171.15	213.3	25
Sweden*	102.86	107.7	5
UK	475.92	518.8	9

* New Union states average growth is 9.5% compared to GNP of current states of 16%
Source OECD

But has the single market brought the benefits expected? The 1988 Cecchini Report to the European Commission suggested that GDP would grow within the Union by 5 per cent. This has been more like ½ per cent. Some of the reasons for this include:

- omission of telecommunications and energy from the single market requirements;
- missed deadlines; passports still remain;

- transitions;
- VAT is due for review in 1996, air transport 1997 and direct access to the Stock Exchanges of Portugal, Spain and Greece is delayed until 1999 for foreign banks;
- some detailed industrial standards are not in place;
- state aid still distorts the market;
- national bias; particularly in public procurement.

THE DECISION-MAKING BODIES

The main decision-making bodies of the European Union are: the Commission; the Council of Ministers; the Court of Justice; the Parliamentary Assembly; and the Economic and Social Committee. In addition, there are said to be 2,000 committees, subcommittees and working parties.

The Commission

Commissioners are appointed by the member governments for four-year renewable terms, and are resident in Brussels. The main duty with which they are entrusted is to make proposals for Community action to the Council of Ministers. The President and Vice-President are chosen from amongst the 14 Commissioners and hold their offices for two-year renewable terms. The UK, West Germany, France and Italy each nominated two Commissioners, whilst the smaller states, Belgium, Holland, Ireland, Denmark and Luxembourg, nominated one each. Spain is to nominate two, and Portugal and Greece one each.

Each Commissioner is responsible for a portfolio, although some will carry more than one portfolio. Each has a private office (cabinet) to which he makes the appointments. Invariably, the members appointed are of the same nationality as the Commissioner. His deputy is known as the *chef du cabinet*. Beneath the Commissioner, there will be one or more Director General – similar to the permanent head of a ministry – who is responsible for a broad policy area, and he will, in turn, have below him Directors and Heads of Division.

The need for Commissioners to be impartial at all times is enshrined in the Treaty of Rome (Article 157) which requires that Commissioners 'shall neither seek nor take instruction from any Government or from any other body'. However, as the Commission only employs 11,000 staff (including translators, interpreters and some 2,600 in the separate scientific and technological Joint Research Centre) – as against perhaps 20,000 for a British Ministry – it is not hard to see that the

Commission can only hope to be effective if the governmental departments of its member states agree to administer its policies. If the Commissioners approve of the draft directive drawn up by a Directorate-General, after any necessary amendments, it is then proposed by the Commission as a draft directive to the Council of Ministers. This gives member states, through the Council of Ministers, the final say on whether the directive becomes law or not. It can, however, take years before legislation is accepted and becomes law.

The Council of Ministers

The Council of Ministers consists of a minister from each member-state government, and the ministers change according to the subjects on the agenda. Ministers represent the interests of their own governments, but try to arrive at agreements which are in the European Union's interest. There is a system of qualified voting so that France, West Germany, Italy and the UK have ten votes each; the Netherlands, Belgium and Greece five votes; Ireland and Denmark three; and Luxembourg two. For a qualified majority, 45 votes are required, but when the Council votes on a proposal that does not emanate from the Commission, then, in addition, the support of six states is also necessary. The Council of Ministers meets only for a certain number of days in the year, and is not resident in Brussels. Each member state takes a six-month turn to chair Council meetings, a national minister of foreign affairs being President of the Council during that period. There is a small permanent staff in Brussels, but the main preparatory work is undertaken by the ambassadors and their embassy staff.

The ambassadors or representatives act as a link between the member countries and the European Union. They meet in the Committee of Permanent Representatives (known as CORE-PER), prepare agendas and agree non-contentious proposals, so that when the ministers attend much has already been agreed and only matters still in dispute need to be negotiated.

The European Council is a meeting of 'the heads of state and government' although, in fact, the only head of state who attends is the president of France, the other countries being represented by their prime ministers. It takes place twice a year and contentious issues which have not been resolved at the Council of Ministers are discussed in the European Council. It is the heads of government who have the authority not only to impose unpopular decisions but also to convince their opposing political forces in their own countries of the need for such decisions. At the end of each Council a communique is issued, giving the broad outline of what has been agreed.

The Court of Justice

The Court of Justice is the ultimate interpreter of the treaties on which the EU is based and the final arbiter of disputes concerning secondary legislation whenever there is a query or disagreement about the meaning of a particular regulation, directive or decision. It is situated in Luxembourg with a staff of 460. There are 11 judges, each appointed for six years. Hearings are in public, but deliberations are private. A judge can only be removed by the unanimous vote of his colleagues to the effect that he is no longer capable of carrying out his duties. A quorum consists of seven judges; there must be an odd number sitting and decisions are reached by simple majority. The Court produces its own reports containing the basic facts of the case, the summing up by the Advocate-General and the judgement. Companies on whom the Commission has imposed fines may appeal to the Court. The Court also gives preliminary rulings for the benefit of national courts. It may proceed against member states if a member state is not fulfilling its legal obligations. It reviews the legality of Community acts and it settles disputes.

The Parliamentary Assembly

Until 1981 the European Parliament held one-third of its sessions in Luxembourg and two-thirds in Strasbourg, in Eastern France. In 1981 it decided to hold no more sessions in Luxembourg, and this was upheld by the Court of Justice. However, more than three-quarters of the parliamentary secretariat of approximately 2,600 are based in Luxembourg which means that they have to travel between the two points regularly.

The first direct elections to the European Parliament were held in June 1979. There are 434 members of the European Parliament who control 15 important committees which scrutinise Commission proposals and prepare reports. They have the right to dismiss the government, ie the Commissioners, provided over half the members vote in favour of this. They also have the final vote on a part of the European Community's budget allocation, and can reject the budget as a whole. They give an opinion, which is not binding, on European laws sent from the Commission to the Council of Ministers.

The Economic and Social Committee

The Economic and Social Committee is purely consultative. Its membership is appointed for four years and currently numbers 156: for example, 24 from France, West Germany and the UK; 12 from Belgium and the Netherlands; 9 from Denmark and Ireland; and 6 from Luxembourg. The spectrum of its membership is broad and includes producers, workers, farmers, transport operators and merchants as well as personnel from the professions, universities, consumer organisations and other appropriate interest groups. Its members are selected by the Council from lists submitted by member states. No particular importance is assigned to its role. Its functions are more akin to an in-house opinion poll for the Council and Commission. Its decisions are reached in open debate in full sessions, rather than by lobbying.

THE LEGAL PROCESSES

Although the European Union's infrastructure is now able to cope with the political intent and the workload required to achieve the 1992 objectives, just under half of the proposed legislative measures put forward by the European Commission have been adopted by the Council of Ministers. It is still possible to influence the outcome of the laws, to lobby for a particular cause or to seek redress where unfair barriers to trade still remain. For this an understanding of the legal process is necessary.

Basically, the legal process consists of four main procedures:

1. The Commission drafts a proposal which it submits to the Council.
2. The Parliament and the Economic and Social Committee (ECOSOC) consider the proposal and formulate an opinion. Amendment may be required by the Commission.
3. The Council of Ministers, taking the opinions of the Parliament and ECOSOC into account, formulate a common position and the proposal is returned to the Parliament for a second reading.
4. If the Parliament agrees with the Council, then it may adopt the proposal by qualified majority voting.

This is known as the Co-operation Procedure and was made possible by the Single European Act. Before that, the Council of Ministers considered proposals which were then adopted by

THE CO-OPERATION PROCEDURE

Figure 2.1 The enactment of an EU Directive

Note The DTI's 'Brussels can you hear me' is a good place to start any campaign of influence unanimity or not at all. Agreement at Maastricht expanded the Co-operation Procedure to most areas with the exception of agriculture, trade and competition policy. A new negative assent and third reading procedure will apply for the Single Market education, environment frameworking programmes, research and culture. This process sets up a conciliation committee between the council and Parliament if they fail to reach agreement, and allows the Parliament a final right to block legislation if they are not happy.

There will also be strengthened provisions for achieving financial control in the European Union with an enhanced role for the EU Court of Auditors, and for the Parliament to call the Commission to account.

There are four different sorts of legislative meaures:

1. *Regulations*, which are laws binding on all member states. They can be adopted by the Council of Ministers and the Commission. No national laws are required.
2. *Directives*, which define the end result, but allow each nation to introduce its own legislation to achieve the goal.
3. *Decisions*, which are similar to regulations and are binding on whom they address.
4. *Recommendations*, which are not law, and therefore not binding.

Pre-lobbying

Lobbying can be conducted at all stages of the legislative process. Obviously, the first step is to lobby at the Commission before draft proposals are produced. The Department of Trade and Industry (DTI) (UK) is prepared to release the names of civil servants who can help in certain areas. Lobbying organisations or trade associations can help with direct lobbying.

As in Britain, lobbying can be done through members of the European Parliament, or representation may be made to the other consultative organ, the Economic and Social Committee. The other route, albeit rather closer to the actual decision, is the Committee of Permanent Representatives, where the working parties for the Council of Ministers are formed to review the Council proposals.

Post-lobbying

The DTI have produced a booklet entitled *The Single Market: Europe Open for Business* which describes the criteria for making a complaint that the European Union rules are working unfairly. It comments:

'The European Court of Justice has also laid down broad guidelines that any rules enacted by member states which are capable of hindering, directly or indirectly, actually or potentially, intra-community trade are covered by Article 30 (establishing the principle that member states cannot maintain quantitative restrictions, or measures which have the equivalent effect, on products from other member states). The measures prohibited include any discrimination between home produced and foreign goods, onerous technical standards or testing procedures, burdensome labelling requirements, unequal taxation regimes, over-rigid pricing or profit margin controls, requirements for import licences or similar procedures, and many other obstacles.'

The DTI is prepared to take up cases of unfair barriers to trade where UK firms face them in other member states. It will also give advice for companies facing what they believe to be unfair trading practices.

USEFUL ADDRESSES

Lobbying (pre-)

Department of Trade and Industry
1–19 Victoria Street
London SW1H OET
Tel: The DTI Hotline 081-200 1992

Unfair practices

Single Market Compliance Unit
Department of Trade and Industry
Room 602
123 Victoria Street
London SW1E 6RB
Tel: 071-215 6703

General information on EU matters can be obtained from the Commission's UK offices:

Headquarters
200 Rue de la Loi
B-1049 Brussels
Tel: 010 322 235 111

8 Storey's Gate
London SW1P 3AT
Tel: 071-973 1992

Windsor House
9–15 Bedford Street
Belfast BT2 7EG
Tel: 0232 240708

4 Cathedral Road
Cardiff CF1 9JG
Tel: 0222 371631

7 Alva Street
Edinburgh EH2 4PH
Tel: 031-225 2058

Information about the European Parliament may be obtained from:
The European Parliament Information Office
2 Queen Anne's Gate
London SW1H 9AA
Tel: 071-222 0411

Information on Centres for European Business Information, including Small and Medium Enterprises Task Force may be obtained from:

Belfast	Tel: 0232 491031
Birmingham	Tel: 021-454 6171
Bradford	Tel: 0274 754262
Brighton	Tel: 0273 220870
Bristol	Tel: 0272 737373
Cardiff	Tel: 0222 229525
Dublin	Tel: (010) 353 695011
Exeter	Tel: 0392 214085
Glasgow	Tel: 041-221 0999
Hull	Tel: 0482 465940
Inverness	Tel: 0463 234121
Leeds	Tel: 0532 439222
Leicester	Tel: 0533 554464
Liverpool	Tel: 051-298 1928
London	Tel: 071-828 6201
	071-489 1992
Maidstone	Tel: 0622 696126

Manchester   Tel: 061-236 3210
Mold   Tel: 0352 2121
Newcastle-upon-Tyne   Tel: 091-261 5131
Norwich   Tel: 0603 625977
Nottingham   Tel: 0602 222414
Sheffield   Tel: 0742 532126
Slough   Tel: 0753 77877
Southampton   Tel: 0703 832866
Stafford   Tel: 0785 59528
Telford   Tel: 0952 588766

For a comprehensive list of services and contacts the DTI Single
Market *Guide to Sources of Advice* and *Brussels can you hear
me* are very useful and free.

3
MARKETING OPPORTUNITIES IN A UNITED EUROPE

The specifics of international marketing will apply equally well to the harmonised European Community post-1992. The cultural and social influences will remain prominent, but the problems and inefficiencies of excessive red tape should disappear; closed public procurement will be finished and a plethora of other product regulations will be standardised.

The completion of the European internal market should achieve one main objective: significant reduction in costs to the consumer. This will be achieved in three main ways:

1. Through economies of scale in product, and businesses rationalising their own organisations.
2. The more open market competitiveness will result in a greater requirement to achieve and retain market share.
3. There will be increased innovation to match consumer needs. As technology itself responds to the free-market atmosphere, consumer-oriented marketing strategies will be the order of the day. Those unable to react will fail.

Potential price falls to the consumers' advantage cover a wide range of products and services. For instance, pharmaceutical prices could fall by 52 per cent in Germany, 40 per cent in the UK; office machine instrumentation could produce a 27 per cent saving in Italy; telephones a 20 per cent saving in Belgium; financial services 34 per cent in Spain and 23 per cent in Belgium.

Companies themselves can look forward to healthier profits for the following reasons:

- lower input costs;

- responsiveness to profit through:

  (a) utilisation of production capacity
  (b) the use of best practice production techniques;

- removal of non-tariff barriers;
- cross-frontier research and development.

The successful company will be an efficient company and will enjoy the profit rewards even when prices fall. Paolo Cecchini, in his influential study *The Benefits of a Single Market* concluded: 'EC market integration heralds a prospect of rich pickings to be earned, not inherited.'

WHICH INDUSTRIES STAND TO WIN?

In an earlier edition of this book, a number of industrial and commercial sectors were identified as most likely to be beneficially assisted by the movement towards harmonisation and standardisation. However, by the end of 1993 only 38 per cent of internal market measures had been implemented in all member states. The UK and Denmark led the field, with 90 per cent and 94 per cent respectively of the directives implemented. The same is true in the wider context of community law. Here again, Denmark and the UK have led but France and the Netherlands have also enacted over 90 per cent of the directives. Given this far from single market market-place, how have some of these previously identified sectors fared?

1. High Technology and Telecommunications

Great hopes were expressed for this sector in expected gains through inter-operability and compatibility. The work on setting common standards which are indicated by 'CE' markings (the Union mark of conformity for all EU and EFTA countries) has progressed well. A recent directive consolidated the discrepancies between EU markings on pressure valves, toys, construction products, electro-magnetic compatibility, machinery, non-automatic weighing instruments, medical devices, gas appliances, telecommunication terminal equipment, hot water boilers and low voltage electronic equipment. These changes should be implemented by January 1995.

Harmonisation, however, has not given the impetus to research and development which would be needed to keep Europe ahead of its competitors. In 1991 the EU countries devoted 1.96 per cent of GDP to research and development, compared with 2.74 per cent in the US and 2.87 per cent in Japan. By the measure of their share of the US patent market, EU companies have declined since 1980 with Asian and Japanese countries making massive expansions. There are a number of companies, however, which are exceptions to this decline within Europe, and these include Siemens (Germany), Philips (Netherlands) and Ericsson (Sweden).

In telecommunications, the Commission is driving rather slowly towards a totally liberalised market. They have backed off from the original targets of 1994 for resale and third party traffic on private networks, and 1996 for cross-border telephone services, pushing the dates to the year 2000. Through consultation with telecom operators, governments and equipment suppliers, the Commission has basically given Union members a free hand. There is a green paper due out by the end of 1994, discussing the future regulation of the public telecom network infrastructure and cable television networks.

Progress has been made on creating a single market in earth station equipment and harmonisation procedures for certification, testing, marketing, quality assurance and product surveillance.

2. Pharmaceuticals and Chemicals

The expected competitive opportunities that the single market could have brought to these industries have, for the most part, been realised. The commission has made substantial progress on product authorisation, pricing and patent protection. It has brought advertising, promotion and distribution into the harmonisation process. These measures have made the sector more competitive and removed much of the national level distortion on supply. The establishment of a European Medicines Agency has helped. Today, the Union is the world's biggest producer of prescription drugs, but the squeeze on prescription drugs from over stretched governmental health budgets creates challenges for this sector. New, innovative products are required capable of generating volume growth. The prime area of growth will thus be in generic and over-the-counter medicines, whose market share will continue to grow as governments' cost containment on health programmes bites. The recognition of the global nature of this market has also to be recognised with the establishment of International Conferences on harmonisation.

Regarding chemicals, the European Chemicals Bureau has been set up and intends to be fully operational in 1996. It has the specific task to assist in classification, packaging and labelling of dangerous substances.

3. Food and Drink

The fears of a politically correct sausage or can of beans have not been realised in the process of food harmonisation within the Union. There still is considerable debate on food additives, sweeteners and colourings. On the whole, the directives have led to responsible hygiene and health driven controls, which has facilitated the single market by giving confidence to consumers in non-production countries. A European food inspectorate, which would include the training of food inspectors, quality standards for laboratories and testing methods, is currently being debated by the Commission, but will need additional finance to be found before it begins its work. The discussion surrounding VAT on alcoholic drinks has also to be harmoniously, if temporarily, resolved although the national idiosyncrasies have caused, in the UK at least, concern at the flow of less expensive wines and beers into the country after the loosening of border controls.

4. Manufacturing

Any expected benefits from harmonisation have accrued to those sectors which use low technology, such as Italian textiles. In fact the areas which have gained greatest world competitiveness have been; wood processing, ethyl alcohol, cotton manufacturing and leather tanning. The worst areas have been in computers, office equipment, medical equipment and motor components. The danger of a low technology strategy is not only losing out to future markets but, by not seeking a particular niche, Europe can get caught between the high technology economies and those where labour costs are considerably lower than in the community. Indeed, the threats to this sector come from those manufacturers who can attract a mass market. Some progress has been made in world competition however, by Union countries in the last five years. During that period, of the top 200 industrial groups, European countries have increased by 8 per cent, while the US has fallen by just over 11 per cent.

5. Transport

The advantages from cross-border liberalisation include; access to new markets, harmonisation of documentation, road taxation and tolls, which have all contributed to a more efficient market. It is estimated that these changes have contributed a 3 per cent saving in time taken moving goods around Europe as cross-border bureaucracy has been removed.

Major infrastructure projects such as the Channel tunnel between France and the UK, and links between Denmark and Sweden, have improved the transport networks. The Channel Tunnel project is, in fact, the costliest piece of infrastructure in Europe and, although it will be ready in 1994, the high speed link to London is unlikely to be finished before 2002. There have been Alpine crossing improvements both within Switzerland and between Austria and Italy.

A new dimension to the European infrastructure projects has been the need to improve East-West linkage. The transport infrastructure costs, for instance, in the unified German Republic have been estimated at DM 200 billion.

In air transport, competition has reduced costs and increased competitiveness. Air traffic control systems have been harmonised both in terms of equipment and conduct. This sector is perhaps more obviously global than other transport systems, and international rather than pan-European mergers seem to be the direction of most strategic activities.

6. Retailing

Retailing employs about 17 per cent of the Union's workforce, and accounts for between 17 per cent of the GNP in Belgium to 35 per cent in Greece. Europe's failure, with a few exceptions, to develop powerful, international retail brands, could see it overrun by US companies such as McDonald's maximising economies of scale and scope. The fragmented nature of the European market is perhaps the cause for the lack of development, due to the different cultures, languages and tastes, but cross-border scepticism has not helped the emergence of this market. Nor have the remaining domestic laws which, in France, Belgium and Germany, restrict the size of retail development. There are exceptions, and cross-border retailers such as Carrefour, Promodes and Ikea have overcome both formal and artificial barriers to achieve substantial sales outside of their home markets.

7. Services

The decline in manufacturing has been more than matched by the growth in services inside the Union. The service sector is now Europe's largest source of employment. The outlook is for a continuing fall in factory jobs and a squeeze on public sector pay throughout Europe, leaving services as one of the few areas where job creation is possible. However, the forces of global competition show the sector to be less efficient in banking and air transport than the US which, in the short-term, can be sheltered by national barriers, but in the long-term will require companies to increase productivity. The impact of the single market has been reasonably good for financial professional business services and transport, but poor in energy supply and air transport.

8. Financial Services

The single market has been successful in harmonising consumer financial service markets but, as yet, the benefits of competitive forces have not been felt within the consumer markets. Indeed in the capital markets some of the issues have not yet been faced. Perhaps one of the most important issues is the fragmented nature of the various security trading centres within Europe. Although producing competition, it could be that one market would increase liquidity and give strength of action as a single force against the major global competitors of Japan and the USA. Since the liberalisation of the insurance, banking and investment markets, the focus of European attention has been on investor protection and compensation schemes.

The conclusions which can be drawn are that through the single market process, the industrial sectors have become inward-looking without remembering that their businesses are part of a complex world economic environment. The answer was harmonisation: now it is to breach the widening research and technological divide between Europe and the other major trading blocks.

4
STRATEGIES FOR COMPETING IN THE EUROPEAN UNION

THE CURRENT SCENE

Given the opportunities which the single market presents, and having considered the risk and the profit potential, how do companies begin a European marketing initiative?

The prospect may seem daunting, but closer analysis of the skills and knowledge required to commence activities will help in seeing opportunities; constant research in an ever-changing market place (and a vast market place at that) will bring things more into focus.

Every member state has recognised the importance of a truly open market. To ensure that the Single Market is understood and capitalised upon, each State has undertaken projects to help not only their own business people but member nationals as well. An initial approach to the relevant country's agency should be the first port of call. Chambers of Commerce in each member state have also started their own initiatives, and again constructive help is available. However, before commencing, it is important first to identify the target best suited to your products/services. Therefore knowledge of each country, its purchasing needs, consumer trends, etc, should be compared with your current and/or proposed service/product and analysed.

The European Union covers a vast geographical area, spread over 2,253,000 square km, with a population in excess of 320 million. But the market, at least for consumer goods, is much more concentrated than these figures imply. Over three-fifths of the European Union's population and its Gross National Product is found in a relatively small area, see Figure 4.1 on page 38. This 'Golden Triangle' generates some five to six times more GNP than the areas bordering on the Mediterranean Sea.

Figure 4.1 The 'Golden Triangle' of the EU
Source Butterworths, 1983

Thus, by closely identifying geographical regions of interests, the problem of scale can be reduced (to some extent) to target clearly the areas which can then form the basis for further market expansion.

The nature of political risk in the Union is in the attitude towards investment and industry. In the UK, for example, the Monopolies Commission needs to be consulted on major sector take-overs or mergers regarding the impact of change on UK consumers. In the context of the European market, the Commission also has to be consulted with regard to large investments, mergers or take-overs which could affect market positions and conduct of trade. (The decision-making bodies of the Community and the role they have in opportunities to undertake profitable business initiatives are discussed in Chapter 2.)

Large companies control over 50 per cent of the European Union's total sales. Europe's 50 largest companies alone account for approximately 25 per cent of these sales. So, where does this leave smaller companies? Competitive advantages in timing and costs have always favoured the smaller company which can adapt quickly often leaving their larger competitor out in the cold. But more importantly, the concept of the European Union helps.

The foundation of the European Union is free trade, and so any business strategy which relies upon market-sharing, price fixing, exclusive purchase and exclusive or selective distribution agreements could fall foul of the Commission's regulations. However, the Commission has created a Business Co-operation Network – the small and medium-sized business task force – to enable organisations to find contacts for collaboration. It has several channels for disseminating information: Euro-Info Bulletins, Target 1992, Euro-Information Centres and the Business Co-operation Network (B–C Net). In the UK, details of all these services can be obtained from your local DTI office, or from the DTI Hotline on 071-200 1992.

Euro-Information Centres, of which there are 39 in Europe (four in the UK), provide an interface between businesspeople and the Commission, providing advice and answering questions on all aspects of the single European market. The B–C Net is a computerised network system that will eventually link small businesses with each other, with business consultants, banks, etc. The aim is to promote co-operation so that smaller businesses can compete with large companies on a more equal footing.

Strategic directions

Each state in which the company aims to operate will further complicate its marketing operations. A firm's well-thought-out corporate direction is critical to success. Arriving at any decision requires careful analysis and the following must be addressed:

- a corporate mission statement;
- set objectives;
- audit of research;
- option assessment: organic growth, acquisition, collaboration;
- evaluation of the realities of the company's position: what it is aiming for – a competitive edge, a market-dominant position, innovation?
- a plan for success.

For firms, it will not be simply a matter of opportunities; there will be disadvantages too. Their own domestic markets are sure to be affected as other European Union firms expand beyond their own national borders. Neither will it be only European competitors; foreign companies (particularly the Japanese) are also being attracted by the harmonised market. The turbulence that can be created in almost all industries' traditional bases will require companies to create defensive strategies as well as expansive ones. Before setting a programme for Europe, five key points should be reviewed in building a secure base and protecting it from predatory companies:

1. Doing something is better than doing nothing – at the very least, undertake strategies which will increase the cost of entry into your own home market for foreign competitors.
2. Find a strong market position to defend, and do not retrench. Retrenching weakens the company's ability to maintain competitiveness.
3. Defend in-depth those areas of business critical to the company's success and survival. This can be achieved, for example, by denying competitors segments and customers upon whom their entry to the market depends.
4. Attack competitors' weaknesses in terms of service, product range and marketing flexibility.
5. Protect the company's unity; weakness gives an advantage to competitors, unity gives confidence to the company and to customers alike.

The President of the Commission, Monsieur Jacques Delors, has devised a paper on growth, competitiveness and employment. Within it, he acknowledges that the hype of the pre-1992 single market may have contributed to the recession during the early 1990s experienced throughout Europe. Delors' paper has been criticised as offering nothing more than security for workers in jobs, and no competitive strategy at all to bring about higher employment and economic recovery.

THE IMPACT ON BUSINESSES IN THE COMMUNITY

Human resources

It will be enormously advantageous for businesses to have personnel who can not only negotiate successfully in a customer's own language, but who are also sensitive to cultural differences. These people need not necessarily be in senior management positions. In the UK for example, only about 4 per cent of management would claim proficiency in business French, but proficiency increases in key posts such as switchboard operators. Recruiting practices may change in response to the facility to recruit across borders. Organisations will need to review their training programmes in the light of the new opportunities presented in the European Union.

The high cost and low flexibility of European workers has impaired the competitiveness of European business. Even though Europe had higher unemployment and lower private sector employment during the 1980s, its average wage costs, rather than falling, have increased by about 4 per cent per annum, against Japanese and American almost zero levels. This is changing where the lower wage Southern European countries have made efforts to improve their flexibility and keep wage costs under control. The economic debate surrounding the Social Chapter continues to vex governments. Education now is a prime issue. To keep up in this competitive world, core workers need sound basic education and training. Europe is better than the USA on this matter, but worse than Japan. Higher education also needs to be improved, with about 30 per cent of European Union adults attending university, compared with about 70 per cent in the United States.

Increasing attention is being paid to higher education as the source of entrants to the higher levels of the labour market. Continental degree courses are typically longer than in the UK, lasting four to six years. Vocational subjects such as engineering, business studies and law nearly always include substantial work placements. Recruitment reflects the need for vocationally-trained personnel, and very few untrained graduates are sought in such member states as the Netherlands, Spain, West Germany and the Republic of Ireland.

If continental graduate recruits are sought, the harmonisation of mobility of law and mutual recognition help. Reaching these graduates will be more difficult in France and Germany, for instance, than in the UK. Recruitment is mainly carried out through personal links with academics, student work placements, direct advertising in newspapers and journals and the national employment services. Graduates are also more inclined to make speculative applications direct to companies. In general, continental graduates are older than UK graduates, and as such will require different training programmes and, usually, more senior positions.

Despite opinion to the contrary, the UK is doing something about language training for industry through the setting up of 20 'Language Export Centres' (LECs). These have been set up to help education and industry by attempting to resolve the language problems. One central telephone centre (on 071-934 0888) gives information as to the location of the LECs around the UK. These centres help to evaluate the strategic needs of organisations and then, with the assistance of the academics, provide linguistic training solutions. They are profit-making organisations.

Marketing and production

Strategic positioning of products and services may have to be reconsidered, not only in the light of the new opportunities, but also of the emerging threats. It is in the areas of research and development, distribution, purchasing, and finance and accounting that the major impacts will occur.

FINANCE FROM THE COMMUNITY

The European Union's budget includes a number of funds, such as the Social Fund and the Regional Development Fund, which promote European Union objectives by financing suitable projects. European Union financing can take the form of grants, low-interest loans, or participation in contracts funded by the European Union. More financing opportunities are available from the European Investment Bank.

However, the operations of the funds and institutions are governed by complex and changing regulations and European Union objectives. To help ascertain the acceptability of an applicant for finance, the Commission of the European Communities publishes a guide to grants and loans. European Union financing has eight main purposes:

1. Employment and training.
2. Agriculture and fisheries.
3. Regional development.
4. Economic development.
5. Energy.
6. Coal and steel.
7. Developing countries.
8. Research and development.

In addition, funds are available for such projects as education, culture and transport.

Information on European Union financing is available in the booklet entitled *Finance from Europe*, and can be obtained from 8 Storey's Gate, London SW1P 3AT (tel: 071-973 1992).

Structural Funds

The EU offers funds which are aimed to counter the risks of

regional imbalances resulting from market liberalisation. The five main objectives of these structural funds are:

1. Promoting the structural adjustment of regions whose development is lagging behind others in the Union.
2. Assisting in converting areas seriously affected by industrial decline.
3. Combating long-term unemployment.
4. Facilitating occupational integration of young people.
5. Speeding up reforms in the Common Agricultural Policy.

Taken together, the three structural funds: European Regional Development; the European Agricultural Guidance and Guarantee; and the European Social Fund, had a budget of 17.6 billion ECUs in 1992. The post-Maastricht emphasis on political and monetary union led to the creation of a fourth fund, the Cohesion Fund. The purpose of this was to assist the poorer member states to adjust to the changes. The countries most likely to benefit are Ireland, Greece, Portugal and Spain.

The European Social Fund

Non-repayable grants for certain employment and training, retraining, resettlement and job creation schemes are available from the European Social Fund. Applications for these grants are only eligible if the scheme assists a group of people or a type of operation within one of the Fund's 'areas of intervention'.

The European Agricultural Guidance and Guarantee Fund

The European Agricultural Guidance and Guarantee Fund (EAGGF, also known as FEDGA) has two sections. The Guarantee section provides support for agricultural products; the Guidance section supports a number of schemes to improve agriculture. The largest part of Guidance section funds is used to underpin national schemes to encourage structural development and to support agriculture in the less favoured areas.

The European Regional Development Fund

The European Regional Development Fund is intended to help eliminate the disparities in levels of development and wealth between different regions. The Fund goes hand-in-hand with national policies aimed at stimulating the economic development of underdeveloped regions by:

- the provision of financial incentives (grants, loans, tax exemptions, etc) to businesses to encourage them to settle in these areas to create jobs;
- the development of infrastructures to enhance the development of these areas and attract investors.

The European Investment Bank

The European Investment Bank (EIB) is the European Union's own bank, providing long-term finance for capital investments meeting European Union priority economic policy objectives. Established by the Treaty of Rome, the EIB is both a European Union institution, with the task of promoting European integration, and a bank, raising the bulk of its fund on capital markets, and lending the proceeds to projects meeting its eligibility criteria.

Finance for Energy

One of the European Union's primary objectives is to ensure adequate supplies of energy for its future development. Financial support for projects conforming with this objective is available in a number of forms. Research funds are offered for both nuclear and non-nuclear research from a wide range of perspectives. The European Commissioner is the best source of information.

The European Coal and Steel Community

The European Coal and Steel Community treaty authorises the Commission to grant loans with an interest rate subsidy to certain investment projects in the coal and steel regions, and to certain low-cost housing schemes. Grants may also be awarded to help the resettlement or redeployment of coal and steel workers, and financial assistance is also available to help technical, social or medical research within the industry. Applications must relate to an investment which has not yet started and can be completed within three years of the date of finance.

Aid for research and development

The European Union research action programmes include three forms of research work:

- Directly-managed research carried out at the four establishments of the European Union's Joint Research Centre.

- Contract research paid for (normally at a level of about 50 per cent) by the Commission and carried out by research organisations in member states.
- Co-ordination of research actions financed and carried out by research organisations in member states, and also frequently in European non-member countries. The Commission has a co-ordinating role, but makes no financial contribution except towards the cost of certain studies and the maintenance of the co-ordination machinery. The Commission awards research grants on a competitive basis. Priority areas for research and technological development are agreed in a 'Framework Programmes for Research and Development'. The third framework runs until 1994 and the fourth takes over until 1998. Included within the fourth framework are the following priority activities: co-operation with non-EU countries and international organisations; dissemination of R & D results; and training and mobility allowances for researchers. A budget of 14.7 billion ECUs has been proposed for the fourth framework.

Miscellaneous funds

The Commission also offers funds for information technology/communications, environmental, bio-technology/health-care, and agriculture and fisheries research.

Education

There is no European Union education fund. A limited number of pilot projects have been initiated in connection with the transition from school to work and the education of the children of migrant workers.

Transport

Transport infrastructure investment may qualify for assistance, provided the project is of European Union interest. The projects most likely to qualify are those situated on major international axes and which are designed to facilitate the movement of goods and passengers within the European Union.

Cultural programme

A limited number of pilot projects are initiated and funded by the European Union in accordance with its cultural programme to improve vocational training and to stimulate employment in the cultural sector. There are also grants available for the conservation of the EU's architectural heritage.

Other funds

The Commission has very small funds which it can use at its discretion to grant subsidies to:

- Higher education institutions setting up a programme of value to European integration.
- Groups, movements, circles or activities of a European nature.
- Non-governmental organisations pursuing humanitarian aims and promoting human rights.

These funds are managed by the Secretariat-General of the Commission in Brussels.

HELP FROM THE COMMUNITY FOR SMALL- TO MEDIUM-SIZED ENTERPRISES

Central to the development of an active and successful free market in Europe is the small- to medium-sized enterprise (SME) Business Task Force of the European Commission. The SME Task Force was established in 1986 to develop policies for small- and medium-sized businesses. The actual definition of what constitutes an SME is dependent upon the member state; in the UK it is VAT levels, in France the number of employees. European-wide addresses of the organisation's offices in each state are provided in the appendix to this chapter. The following extract, provided by one such unit, explains the function of the units:

'The European Community has embarked on an ambitious series of measures to help small and medium-sized companies. One such action aims to improve the flow of information to SMEs by setting up channels of communication and information on community activities. This will be achieved through the Centres for European Business Information which will not only supply firms with information and advice but also gather their suggestions on requests for specific services. The centres are set up within existing decentralised 'host' organisations in the member states, which have close contact with SMEs, in order to ensure that they can cater for firms' day-to-day needs.

'The Centres will be equipped with a computer-based system which will respond to requests for information on community activities. SMEs will be able to make enquiries on community information at the centres in person, or by post, telex, telefax or phone. For example:

(a) The internal market – the legal, regulatory, social and technical aspects governing intra-community trade and the likely changes following completion of the internal market; opening up public supply contracts, etc.

(b) EU's operational policies – community grants and financial instruments; research and demonstration programmes; sectoral measures; training schemes; regional policy measures and trade relations with non-member states.

'Where applicable, the centres will also provide help on completing application procedures and will co-operate with the EU's information offices on information campaigns directed at a wider public. The activities of the centres also include the organisation of, and participation in, national and international business events such as trade fairs, exhibitions and seminars. they will also stimulate co-operation between business nationally and internationally. The centres will prepare general information sheets and special packs in response to requests for assistance and advice; monitoring of local publications.

'The commission (SME Task Force) will provide the centres with basic community documentation regularly updated and access to EU databases, will be responsible for staff training and will meet part of the marginal costs of opening up the centres with a limited financial contribution in the first year. Within the SME Task Force there is a central structure, staffed with Information Officers, who are on hand to respond to enquiries from SMEs which the centres cannot deal with alone.'

In the UK, the Department of Trade and Industry (DTI) itself helps companies of all sizes to export directly to Europe. The DTI's regional offices are able to offer advice on the Export Initiative's support, which ranges from consultancy support to assistance in exhibiting overseas. The Exports to Europe branch in London is able to provide information on individual markets, and assist with enquiries about import duties, regulations and taxes.

Central to the development of the DTI's programme are the Regional Offices. These co-ordinate the needs of firms and help them to apply for consultancy funding of up to 15 days of a consultant's time. They also advise on the correct department for ad hoc desk-top market research sources. These addresses are also listed on pages 49–50 of this chapter.

A STRATEGIC CHECKLIST FOR THE SINGLE MARKET

- Be aware of legislation and how it could adversely affect your business: be prepared to lobby if necessary. Do not restrict your review to Community countries; non-EU country negotiations can offer even more threats or opportunities.
- Identify what are the major likely changes for your business and conduct an internal audit. *Do not* try to fool yourself as to your readiness.
- Identify and review the likely impact upon:

    (a) potential and existing customers;
    (b) suppliers;
    (c) existing competitors;
    (d) new entrants to your market.

- Evaluate the opportunties which arise to sell products or services in new markets by assessing the viability of entering new markets.
- Set up an overall review strategy for the challenges ahead, testing opportunities and threats against the company's aims and profit projections.

APPENDIX

If you need advice or information about any aspect of exporting to the EU from the UK, contact your regional DTI Office, or speak to an Exports to Europe Branch country desk:

Belgium, Luxembourg	071-215 5486
Denmark	071-215 4397
France	071-215 4762
Germany	071-215 4796
Greece	071-215 5103
Ireland	071-215 4783
Italy	071-215 5103
Netherlands	071-215 4790
Portugal	071-215 5103
Spain	071-215 5624
General EC enquiries	071-215 5336

Or write to:

Exports to Europe Branch
Department of Trade and Industry
66–74 Victoria Street
London SW1E 6SW

UK Department of Trade and Industry's Export Initiative regional centres

Newcastle-upon-Tyne
(North-East)

Stanegate House
2 Groat Market
Newcastle-upon-Tyne NE1 1YN
Tel: 091-232 4722
Fax: 091-232 6742

Manchester
(North-West)

Sunley Tower
Piccadilly Plaza
Manchester M1 4BA
Tel: 061-236 2171
Fax: 061-228 3740

Leeds
(Yorkshire & Humberside)

25 Queen Street
Leeds LS1 2TW
Tel: 0532 443171
Fax: 0532 338301

Nottingham
(East Midlands)

Severns House
20 Middle Pavement
Nottingham NG1 7DW
Tel: 0602 506181
Fax: 0602 587074

Birmingham
(West Midlands)

77 Paradise Circus
Queensway
Birmingham B1 2DT
Tel: 021-212 5000
Fax: 021-212 1010

London
(South-East)

Room 104
Bridge Place
88/89 Eccleston Square
London SW1V 1PT
Tel: 071-215 0571
Fax: 071-828 1109

Bristol

The Pithay
Bristol BS1 2PE
Tel: 0272 272666
Fax: 0202 299494

Scottish Trade Internal

Industry Department for Scotland
120 Bothwell Street
Glasgow G2 7JP
Tel: 041-248 2700

Welsh Office Industry Department

New Crown Building
Cathays Park
Cardiff CF1 3NQ
Tel: 0222 825097

Industrial Development Board for Northern Ireland

IDB House
64 Chichester Street
Belfast BT1 4JX
Tel: 0232 233233
Fax: 0232 231328

5
THE EUROPEAN CONSUMER

POPULATION STRUCTURE

Much has been written about the unified market of 320 million potential consumers; larger than the United States, the Soviet Union or Japan. But it is not spread evenly across the whole geography of the European Union. The UK, Italy, France, Germany and Spain account for 83 per cent of the population. The density of the population measured in persons per square kilometre is greatest in the Netherlands, followed by Belgium, Germany, the UK and Italy. The least densely populated country is the Republic of Ireland. The density obviously varies within member states and basically corresponds to industrial regions or administration centres such as Madrid, Lisbon and Naples. In Spain, there is a concentration in coastal areas, due to the influence of tourism since the late 1960s.

Demographic trends show a decline in the European birth rate since 1960, more pronounced and sustained than in the United States or the Soviet Union. The significance of this is brought more into perspective when the population replacement rate is reviewed against actual births. In only two countries, the Republic of Ireland and Spain, does the birth rate actually match or exceed the population replacement rate. Germany's birth rate is 38 per cent below the replacement rate. The impact on economic, political and social policy for Europe is hard to evaluate; however, continued long-term decline will seriously reduce the market and change consumer purchasing trends. Germany already has a decline in its total population.

The growth rate for the population of Europe is projected to increase (better health care and life expectancy) in the next 15 years, but only by 2 per cent. This leaves an ageing Europe. The economic consequences will be felt increasingly amongst all European states, but perhaps Germany will be worst hit. Here, the population is estimated to decline by 15 million by 2030. In this reduction, the distribution of age structure will also change, moving the over-60s from the 20 per cent they now occupy to 38 per cent and cause a reduction in the under-20s from 20 per cent to 16 per cent.

CONSUMPTION AND PRICES

The ageing of Europe will significantly alter patterns of consumption, production, employment, savings, investments and innovation, but exactly how is still anyone's guess. To illustrate how this change will affect the Union, the number of 65-year olds is likely to grow by 40 per cent between 1990 and 2030. This will amount to over 50 million Western Europeans aged over 65. Even now, a man living within the European Union aged 60 can expect to live until 78 and a woman to 82. This changing age profile has significant consequences for pension and health provision, and it has been estimated that simply to maintain pensions, economic growth in the Union over the next 50 years must be at least 1.5 per cent to keep up with wage inflation.

The focus on what has become known as the 'third age consumer' is attracting considerable attention, particularly from those keen for them to spend their money on leisure, holidays and healthcare. There is also an increase in expenditure on financial services to provide an income for retirement.

As might be expected, there is a wide variation in the Union's cost of living. The table below shows the comparative cost of a basket of basic commodities, allowing for currency differentials. The Mediterranean countries of Portugal, Greece and Spain are the cheapest to live in, while it can cost up to 70 per cent more to live in Germany. This gap is likely to widen by the inclusion of EFTA members. These figures alone illustrate the huge task of bringing a single European social and economic policy into reality.

The EU's rate of growth of consumption of goods fell after the 1973 oil crisis and only fairly recently, in 1982, did it begin to accelerate. In 1987 it matched the world's highest spending (and most wasteful) nation, the United States.

All Europeans obviously do not spend their money in the same way. Spending patterns vary from one country to another. For instance, in Denmark the amount spent on accommodation, communications and recreation is above average. By contrast, in Greece, one of the poorest of the Southern European

Table 5.1 Comparative Prices for a basket of consumer goods and services

	Denmark	France	Germany	Greece	Ireland	Netherlands	Norway	Portugal	Spain	Sweden	UK
Denmark	100	124	92	161	147	120	95	187	154	109	148
France	81	100	100	130	119	97	77	152	124	88	120
Germany	91	112	68	146	133	109	86	170	139	99	134
Greece	62	77	108	100	91	75	59	116	95	68	92
Ireland	98	84	75	110	100	82	65	128	105	74	101
Netherlands	83	103	92	134	122	100	79	156	128	91	123
Norway	105	130	116	169	154	126	100	196	161	114	155
Portugal	53	66	59	86	78	64	51	100	82	58	79
Spain	65	80	72	105	95	78	62	122	100	71	96
Sweden	114	141	101	148	135	110	88	172	141	100	136
UK	68	84	75	109	699	81	65	127	104	74	100

Source: OEED

countries, households spend about twice the average proportion of their income on food, drink and tobacco. The growth areas across Europe are communications and recreation, particularly in Belgium, France, the Netherlands and the UK. Consumption of foodstuffs and clothing is only increasing in Greece.

As spending patterns shift, so too does the relative cost of goods and services. And it is because of this economic shift that the European Union is beginning to build a consumer policy. The impetus for such a move is the opening up of the Union's markets to member states for products from those countries. With such a policy, consumer protection also has to be taken into consideration, both in terms of its positive influence, ensuring confidence and awareness in the consumer to make

Figure 5.1 Comparative consumption patterns across the EU

his purchasing decision and in preventing non-tariff barriers being erected in the name of consumer protection.

CONSUMER PROTECTION

In some respects, consumer protection has been one of the last policy areas to be addressed by the European Union. No mention is made of it in the Treaty of Rome; in fact, it was not until 1972 in Paris that heads of state of governments asked the EU institutions to prepare a programme aimed at strengthening and co-ordinating measures on consumer protection.

Within a few months, the Directorate-General for the Environment, Consumer Protection and Nuclear Safety was set up. In September 1973 the Consumers' Consultative Committee (CCC) was set up, representing the European Bureau of Consumers' Unions (EBCU), the Committee of Family Organisations in the European Communities (Coface), the European Community of Consumer Co-operatives (Euro-coop) and the European Trades Union Confederation (ETUC). Each of these four organisations elects six representatives, and there are nine independent experts.

In 1975, it presented the preliminary programme of the European Economic Community for consumer protection and information policy. Within the programme were contained five basic consumer rights:

- the right to health, protection and safety;
- the right to protection of economic interests;
- the right to redress;
- the right to information and education;
- the right to representation.

A second programme, adopted in 1981, reaffirmed these five rights, and put special emphasis on value for money as a matter of concern for consumers.

The CCC worked hard in the uphill struggle of harmonisation of standards, but with little success. However, the current approach is that the freedom of trade will not have to wait for the completion of technical work on standards. Once the essential health and safety criteria are provided for by EU-wide legislation, the standards of each state will be recognised by the others, and products complying with standards may be traded freely.

This new approach (work is still being undertaken by the European standardisation bodies, CED and Cenelec (the

European Committee for Standardisation and the European Electrotechnical Standardisation Committee, in preparing common standards) was caused by a landmark judgement given by the Court of Justice concerning the *Cassis de Dijon* case. This judgement meant that the free movement of goods did not have to await the establishment of common standards.

Measures have been adopted in three main areas of health and safety:

1. Foodstuffs. These are lists of permitted substances and parity standards have been established for foodstuff additives such as colourings, antioxidants and preservatives. Regulations have been introduced to govern the production of such foods as cocoa, tinned milk and chocolate. Directives have been introduced on the labelling of foodstuffs, specifying in-gredients, quantity and date by which they should be consumed. Drugs and chemicals used for the rapid growth of animals for human consumption, and pecticides, have been banned or restricted.
2. Dangerous substances. Directives control the classification, marketing and labelling of toxic substances. The Community Directive 76/769, issued in 1976, provides for the banning of substances.
3. Pharmaceuticals. The testing, patenting, labelling and marketing of pharmaceutical products are all controlled by EC directives.

In 1984, the Council of Ministers established a system for a rapid exchange of information on dangerous products and substances. This was particularly effective after the Chernobyl disaster.

Although all of the directives are important, and the reader is referred directly to the Commission to ensure the compliance of his products, the most important concern of this chapter is economic safety: the ability of the consumer to determine whether the purchase of certain goods and services can satisfy his needs. The risk shared between supplier and consumer – have I made the right product? Is this product exactly what I want? – has swung in favour of the producer. In the first consumer programme, the Commission recognised this. It states:

'The consumer . . . has become merely a unit in a mass market, the target of advertising campaigns and of pressure by strongly organised production and distribution groups. Mergers, cartels and certain self-imposed restrictions on competitiveness have also created imbalances to the detriment of consumers' (*Source* OJC 92, 1975, page 3)

Throughout 1993, the Council adopted a wide range of amendments to directives concerning consumer protection. These dealt with controls on foodstuffs, direct marketing, safety of toys, construction products, timeshares and even summertime. In July 1993 the Commission published its second action plan for consumers, which covers three years from 1993 to 1995. It has dual aims to consolidate existing legislation and to present new initiatives to raise the level of consumer protection. One of the key areas it attempts to resolve is the use of foreign languages on labelling of foods. Already information requirements have been laid down regarding the quality and characteristics of the products being sold, but now the Commission is interested in encouraging this information to be provided multi-lingually, and particularly in the language of the country of consumption. Indeed, there has been a case in the Court of Justice which clarifies the concept of 'language easily understood by consumers'.

Late in 1993 the Commission adopted a Green Paper on access for consumers to justice and settlements of consumer disputes within the single market. This Paper dealt with unlawful trans-frontier procedures, a mechanism for recording complaints and an evaluation of a pan-European code of conduct for trans-frontier purchases.

ADVERTISING

Advertising harmony and access are critical to the development of a free market. Restrictions on the advertising of individual products can directly affect their exporting prospects. Although individual country practices are to remain, it has been agreed that legislation is needed to regulate advertising to remove and avoid barriers to trade as well as to prevent deception of consumers. A directive adopted in 1984 prohibits misleading advertising, defining this as:

'any advertising which in any way, including its presentation, deceives or is likely to deceive the persons to whom it is advertised or whom it reaches and which, by reason of its deceptive nature, is likely to affect their economic behaviour or which, for these reasons, injures or is likely to injure a competitor.' (*Source* Directive 84/450, OJC 250)

This means that consumers or organisations may, if they believe they were misled, bring a complaint in law or to a competent administrative authority. In the UK, an amendment to law gives full power to this directive. Even more, the burden of proof is not with the consumer, but with the advertiser to prove the truth of his statements. The courts are also empowered to prevent or halt the publication of advertising.

Developments in satellite and cable television have brought a wider problem; that of pan-European broadcasts which, sent from one member state into another, avoids the stricter regulations in the latter state. There is still no formalised Union policy on advertising, so each product sector produces its own legislation. However, there are cross-frontier directives which restrict advertising for tobacco and prescriptive drugs, and directives which deal with the number of commercial breaks and the quota of European national broadcasts on television. There is a third directive dealing with misleading information. Fundamentally this ensures that:

1. Advertising must not offend against prevailing standards of decency and good taste.
2. It must contain no racial or sexual discrimination.
3. It must not be offensive to religious or political beliefs.
4. It must not exploit fear without good reason.
5. It must not encourage behaviour prejudicial to health and safety.

Other harmonisation regulations are being debated and cover such things as children's and comparative advertising. For the most part, the media have remained unregulated.

Direct mail within the Union is restricted by concerns over confidentiality and personal privacy. Two directives cover these areas, which make targeting of customers more difficult as their prior co-operation is required. In the area of sales promotion, regulation is still very much at the national level; money off vouchers are illegal in Spain but not in Germany, and free draws are illegal in the Netherlands. The Commission has been slow to initiate a cohesive policy towards marketing, but this is like to appear as the reality of the single market emerges.

CONTRACT LAW AND DIRECT SELLING

'Purchasers of goods and services should be protected against the abuse of power by the seller, in particular against one-sided contracts, the unfair exclusion of essential rights of contracts, harsh conditions of credit, demands for payment for unsolicited goods and against high pressure selling methods.' (*Source* OJC 1975)

That is how the 1975 initial programme set out the principle of protecting consumer interests. However, as yet very little has been done to redress the balance at present so strongly in the favour of those large institutions which trade just the right side of the member state's laws.

The European Union has taken some action only in regard to direct, doorstep selling. Adopted in 1985 (Directive 85/577, OJC) it deals with the conduct of agents calling uninvited to a consumer's home. The directive provides for a 'cooling-off' period of seven days following the signature of certain contracts, during which period the signatory may cancel the agreement. This right does not apply to contracts of insurance, securities, or mail order sales, or to contracts with a lower value than 60 ECUs.

CREDIT

Access to credit in other member states is to be a very important part of the consumer's post-1992 freedom. A directive adopted in 1986 (Directive 87/102, OJC) provides basic protection by requiring credit agreements to be made in writing and either the cost of the credit or the annual percentage rate of charge to be made clear. Under preparation is the standardisation of the way in which credit charges are expressed. All forms of credit are covered, including personal loans, credit card accounts and permanent credit allowed by suppliers and instalment sales.

SOCIAL CHANGE AND ITS IMPACT ON EUROPEAN MARKETING

This topic is built around the work carried out by Elizabeth H. Nelson in association with RISC (Research into Social Change). She has been able to identify social changes which are truly pan-European.

Although the starting point and speed of change in attitudes of 'Mr Average' from each country differs, consistency in trends appear. Using the RISC European Socio-Cultural map, the position of each country can be plotted. The position of the country on the map depends upon where the bulk of its population falls. For example, more people in France, Italy and Spain live in the northern half of each country, while the UK and the Netherlands have more people living in the southern half. The UK has changed its position in the past five years, moving more rapidly towards the centre than Germany.

Social change is mapped across two axes. The horizontal axis positions information-gathering from close family links and working environments: 'roots'; and a less restricted, more flexible, wider social contact environment based on personal interests developed: 'networking'. People high on this trend have a wider group of social contacts which are regularly changing. Because they seek out groups of people for information, rather than relying on a small number of references, they are usually better informed.

The impact on the promotion of products is important. It could create a move away from major branded campaigns to direct marketing. It is proposed that fewer people are likely to identify with slogans which suggest 'largest' or 'most modern' products, but rather will buy ones which they perceive to possess certain qualities which will meet a particular need. Large multinationals are becoming aware of a need to provide homogenous images where a heterogenous personality would be more appropriate. This is particularly true of American Express's European advertising.

The vertical axis is similar in many ways to Maslow's 'hierarchy of needs'. In the southern section of the map, fixed survival needs still predominate, whilst the northern section is more self-expressive and less nationalistic, with a greater acceptance of and capacity to manage change. For instance, in the late 1940s and 1950s, Europe had a strong commitment to the work ethic. Today with technology allowing more free time, whilst providing increased national prosperity, there is a general decline in the work ethic. This decline has been matched by an increase in the expectation of personal pleasure, greater interest in consumerism and a growing concern for controlling the influence of technology, particularly its impact on the environment. The 'Green' issues are an increasingly influential factor in all European attitudes. They are strongest amongst the young and better educated.

Other trends identified are moves towards:

1. *Polysensuality.* The desire for, say, consumers to smell fresh bread or coffee as well as to consume it.
2. *Open citizenship.* The loss of a degree of sovereignty, with consumers seeing themselves more as European than French,

German or British. The understanding of the economic Europeanisation is growing in the UK, but more slowly than in the rest of Europe: Italy and France are well ahead.

3. *Achievement and risk-taking.* There seems to be a clear trend that people in more demanding and interesting jobs work longer and longer hours, blurring the work/leisure time distinction. A higher level of risk is accepted to gain success. Fashion and 'smart buys' are important to those showing this trend.

4. *Strategic opportunism.* There is a move away from complex, detailed research of business and personal decisions, towards a more aggressive, 'go for it' mentality.

5. *Exploring mental frontiers.* This is the growing feeling that we do not know enough about how we think and feel. This leads to an increasing reliance on emotion and intuition in making decisions.

The map depends upon the acceptance of EU social values. The evidence that some such element exists is in the global marketing successes of multinational brands such as Coca Cola, Walkman, Marlboro and McDonald's. However, understanding social cultural trends helps to fine-tune campaigns in order to achieve better results. Nielsen quotes pasta as an example:

> 'In every European country outside Italy, people who eat pasta frequently tend to be at the forefront of social trends, but people in Italy who eat a lot of pasta are backward on the trends. Therefore, a successful marketing policy for pasta in Italy would be very different from that in other countries.'

There is a convergence of trends amongst those who are at the forefront of change. The similarity of attitude in students, businessmen and professionals across Europe is significantly higher than people in those same countries who live in part of the south-west corner of the RISC map. The marketeer must take advantage of the trends, and apply his knowledge of the direction in which societies are moving. Merely satisfying customer needs is passive. According to Pepsi Cola's John Scully, 'The purpose of marketing now is to anticipate, persuade and influence.'

6
THE UNSPOKEN WORD

In conducting business with fellow Europeans there can be the inevitable problem of language. This is likely to remain the case, certainly for the language-shy British and certain other EU member states, for at least the rest of this century.

Learning European languages has to become an essential part of trading in the future. However, that is only part of the solution. As well as the standard written and spoken word, there is another factor that should not be overlooked – body language, or as the social psychologists call it, non-verbal communication (NVC).

Complications result when people verbally say one thing, but communicate a completely different thing with body language. Which one do you believe? Between people of the same nationality this can be difficult, but in mixed cultures it can be totally confusing. For instance, if an Italian puts his thumb and forefinger on his lips, what does this mean? What it actually signifies is sewing the lips together and he is telling you to be quiet. You might have guessed this, because it is a fairly close universal gesture, ie putting the forefinger on the lip. But what if you were wrong? It could turn out to be very embarrassing.

If there is a conflict between the verbal message and the physical, then generally the social psychologists and body-language experts say that we should trust the physical communication as being the accurate one. However, across nations and cultures it becomes harder to distinguish and separate these differences and understand the nuances – but it is important to be aware where variations may lie.

Therefore, it is not just what people say that is important, but also how they say it, and this is likely to involve body-language in one way or another. It is crucial to be able to interpret and read the true meaning of gestures or expressions.

Fortunately, within Europe, while there are a number of

particular variations or national characteristics, there are, thankfully, many common gestures or expressions which are common ground for all. The variations are most extreme in Northern Europe compared with the Mediterranean area.

FACIAL EXPRESSIONS

The face can convey a multitude of diverse messages, but it is possible to make a generalised summary of these, at least as far as they are likely to affect business transactions. For practical purposes, it is possible to concentrate on the six key emotions of happiness, sadness, anger, disgust, surprise and fear. Across Europe, there is a reasonable closeness of expressions for most of these, though it does become harder to distinguish the difference between fear and surprise.

For Germans, there is some divergence from the more open expressions and there is a moderation or balance between the norms of the expression and the meaning conveyed. This divergence occurs on the following basis.

Table 6.1   Expressions and their meanings

Expression	Meaning
smiling	dominant
raised brows	happy
lowered brows	dominant

For most Europeans, these are fairly closely correlated, but Germans may be somewhat at variance.

The ability of Europeans to decode each others' expressions seems to be good — certainly better than trying to read non-Europeans, for example, the Japanese. In tests carried out, English and Italians scored highest at reading their own national intentions and also each other's.

For the gaze, or what is more normally referred to as eye contact, again European behaviour tends to be fairly commonly held. Europeans seem to be capable of accommodating our mannerisms to the degree which is acceptable and not intimidating to the other partner in the conversation. However, Southern Europeans seem to be more intense here and one notable exception seems to be the Greeks, who are much keener on a continuous eye contact and likely to be offended if your eyes start to wander from theirs. They prefer direct eye contact and because of this it would be difficult to hold a meaningful conversation with a Greek whilst walking side-by-side down the street, or if you were wearing sun-glasses.

Gestures

With regard to gestures, it is reassuring to discover that many of our conventional gestures are universal throughout Europe. These include pointing, shrugging shoulders, patting people on the back, head nodding, thumbs down, clapping, waving and beckoning. However, while the head nod for 'yes' is common, there is some disparity with the head-shake for 'no'. While Northern Europeans recognise the head-shake, in Greece this is replaced by the head-toss.

Generally, there is less use of gestures in Northern Europe and greater use in Southern Europe, with France possibly taking the middle ground.

Another gesture you may come across is the pursed hand. Seldom seen in the UK, this has a number of different meanings throughout Europe; in France, it stands for 'fear', in Greece 'good' and in Italy it signifies a query.

Italian gestures you should look out for are the open hand put in front of the face with fingers and thumb spread. If you see this gesture, it could mean that the business negotiations are not going too well (the sign actually represents 'gaol')! If the Italian starts to make a sign with thumb and fingers put up to the eye forming a monocle, this is a rather scornful way of telling you to watch out – a form of disbelief at what you are saying.

For emotional display, the facial gestures are fortunately fairly common to all, and you will be on reasonably safe ground interpreting that shaking the fist indicates anger; yawning, boredom; touching the face, shame; showing the palm of the hand and lowering the hand, submission.

The North and South divide

Under the heading of 'spatial behaviour', for practical purposes it is helpful to split Europe into the North and South divide. For this, the contact cultures are separated from the non-contact cultures. Broadly speaking, the former are represented by the South, and the latter by the North. For the contact races, there is a stronger tendency to stand closer to people, have more face-to-face contact, touch more often and speak in a louder voice.

For Northern Europeans, it could be necessary to adjust your behaviour to cope with this, and whilst not duplicating their actions at least being able not to be put off by it.

Studies in the past have indicated that the Southern Europeans like to stand much closer to each other than Northern Europeans. This can mean that the Southerners will stand about two feet from each other, but the distance will more likely be over three feet between Northerners. A number of generalisations can be drawn from this which would seem to indicate that the Northern Europeans are less physical than the Southerners.

The same study seems to support this view by considering the interaction as witnessed by touch and the use of the voice. For Southerners, the voice is much louder and there is a greater preponderance of touching, reflecting warmer and more intimate behaviour.

The problems here would seem to focus around trying to seek the right balance with the business relationship; if you stand too far away you may find that your partners see you as distant and unfriendly. On the other hand, if you invade their personal territory you might embarrass them and be seen as intrusive and overfamiliar. As a general rule, it is a good idea to spend a little time trying to observe these differences closely. It is best to take your cue from your host/buyer, but stay alert and be willing to adapt your behaviour as different cultural circumstances demand.

The British are not great 'touchers' and studies have shown that these characteristics are also shared with the Germans and Dutch. However, the Southern Europeans and French are prone to be more expressive. In one study a comparison of touching found that the number of touches per hour made by couples in cafés was 100 for Paris, and zero in London.

SOME EUROPEAN CONTRASTS

The OK sign

In Britain, to signal 'OK, fine', the hand is raised and a circle is made with the thumb and forefinger. In France, that gesture alone means 'zero' or 'worthless'. In Greece, it is an obscene insult to either male or female.

The nose tap

Tapping the side of the nose in Britain is a meaning of secrecy or conspiracy, but in central Italy it signifies 'take care, there is danger, they are crafty'.

Eye touch

This is where the forefinger touches the face just below the eye and pulls the skin downwards, opening the eye wider. In France, it means 'you can't fool me, I see what you are up to'. In Italy, it means 'keep your eyes peeled, pay attention, he's a crook'.

Chin flick

The back of the fingers swept upwards and forwards against the underside of the chin in France means 'get lost, you are annoying me', but in Greece it is not an insult, just a negative 'I don't want any' or 'I cannot'.

Nodding/shaking the head

The nodding and shaking of the head to indicate yes and no are fairly standard, except in Greece where the rhythmical movement of the head from side to side can mean 'yes' rather than 'no'. And for 'no' the Greeks will tilt their heads sharply back and return it less sharply to the neutral posture.

Hand waving

In Britain, the lateral wave dominates, while in France the vertical wave is more usual and in Italy the hidden palm wave, similar to beckoning, replaces both.

7
ON EUROPE, EAST AND WEST

Although economic harmony is not yet established within the traditional 'free' Western European Community, the dramatic and inspiring changes occurring within the Commonwealth of Independent States and their old satellite dependencies has brought a new dimension to a unified, if not federal, Economic Community. The changes have been recent and rapid. It was only in January 1991 that member Governments of the Council of Mutual Economic Assistance (CMEA) disbanded their organisation, and only in October of that year that Poland, Czechoslovakia and Hungary – collectively known as the 'triangle' – declared their intention to seek associate status with the European Community, and subsequently full membership of the Community through integration in the system of European political co-operation. Agreements were initialled in November 1991.

President Havel of Czechoslovakia, opening the first Conference on European Confederation, held in Prague in June 1991, spoke of his vision of Europe where, over the next 15 to 20 years, a confederation of states would be born, doubling the trading opportunities. He put it thus:

'We all know that the whole of Europe, let alone the part which has just rid itself of Communism, cannot gain membership of the European Community the day after tomorrow. But the economic and political areas being created by the EC and EFTA countries should, in their own interests, not be forcibly closed; it should rather be opened up.'

He cautioned, however, 'the unbelievable hopes which have opened up for Europe are mixed with fears, uncertainty and doubt'.

It is indeed a long way for the excited ex-members of CMEA to travel to establish a free market economy and a political stability to facilitate a seamless joining of East and West. However, given substance to the West's verbal encouragement, success should be achieved.

The remainder of this chapter deals briefly with the structures and systems which pertained prior to the break-up of CMEA, particularly with respect to Albania, Bulgaria, Romania – the poorest of the Eastern European states – and to the triangle of Czech and Slovak Federal Republic, Poland and Hungary. The economic relationship with the old Soviet Union is discussed prior to individual country assessments. The changes and the volatility of trading with the member states of the Commonwealth and Yugoslavia are so great that they have not been included in this chapter.

Stalin created CMEA in 1949, and it was forced on the member countries as the economic cornerstone of the Soviet bloc. It had its successes, and it is these very successes that will make transformation to market economies difficult. The system depended on central planning, high demands for energy and the transformation of base resources (supplied by the Soviets) into goods sellable back into the Soviet Union and to the West by member countries. This manufacturing/consumption cycle was made to work by the Soviets subsidising their allies, with little reference to world market-prices. Because no competition existed to sharpen efficiencies within CMEA, member countries became more isolated and technologically backward. This reduced the attractiveness of their goods to the Western markets and threw the countries back on to a greater reliance on the Soviet market-place. However, with the disbanding of the CMEA, the virtual barter system of Soviet resources for Eastern goods stopped dead in its tracks. The move to market prices in hard currencies, for example the dollar rather than the artificial 'transferable rouble', has had a major and painful impact on all CMEA countries. The only short-term winners, if they can be so described, are members of the Commonwealth of Independent States, who can trade their raw resources in hard currencies, whereas their Eastern European satellites are left with inferior goods which are unattractive to Western markets and so are unable to generate the hard currency required to pay for raw resources.

This situation is transitional, if a free market system is pursued, but it will take time and will be painful. The Polish government found out at the end of 1991 that the pace of change demanded by the populace is greater than the evolution proposed by the economists. Help is needed from the West to assist and mitigate some of the hardships, and this is arriving through various organisations. The West's concern is to build a free market infrastructure and retain political stability. Regarding international debt, Eastern Europe is coming in from the cold. In a recent deal Poland agreed to start repaying on debts outstanding, given that its $13 billion commercial debt is written down to 43 per cent of that value. Russia, Hungary and the Czech Republic have all received substantial loans. The internal Stock Market in Poland has been spectacular, showing over 900 per cent growth in 1993 and being the world's best performer. Although not in that league, the Czech market has shown growth of 250 per cent and after difficulties in 1992, Hungary's market has moved ahead by 50 per cent.

Three organisations have been set up to assist the Eastern, or, as they prefer to be termed, Central European countries, and a fourth has been set up by these countries themselves to network their experience and expertise, particularly in respect to the privatisation of their industries. Each of these organisations can provide information on investment and market conditions for industry-specific projects.

International Financial Corporation (IFC)

1818 H Street NW,
Washington DC 20433,
USA
Tel: 202-477 123

This organisation was set up by the World Bank to assist with privatisation and joint ventures in Czechoslovakia, Poland, Yugoslavia and Hungary. It offers advice on foreign investment and internal restructuring.

The European Union PHARE Programme

European Commission Directorate General 1
Rue de la Loi
B-1049 Brussels
Tel: 235-6124/3378

This project was originally set up to give assistance to Hungary and Poland, but is now available to all Central economies. The project is administered and funded from EU budgets. It attempts to support the process of transformation from a centralised system to a market economy. The guide-lines set out an overall framework for the PHARE programme. The central aim of PHARE continues to be to provide assistance for economic reform, structural adjustment and sustainable development in Central Europe, and more particularly to help to convert centralised economies into economies based on market-orientated mechanisms. Assistance under PHARE will remain focused on four priority areas: the restructuring and/or privatisation of state-owned firms, in industry as in agriculture; assistance for the private sector (notably SMEs) and the promotion of private investment and tourism; modernisation of the financial system; and the establishment of a social security system including pro-active employment policies and suitable methods of fighting poverty.

European Bank for Reconstruction and Development (EBRD)

1 Exchange Square
London EC2A 2EH
Tel: 071-338 6000

This bank was set up by the Commission of the EC, 40 other countries including the USA, and the European Investment Bank, to foster the transition towards open market orientated economies and to provide private and entrepreneurial initiatives. The bank held its first annual review meeting in April 1992, where food, textiles, steel and car manufacturing were identified as the areas with the most immediate potential for restructuring and privatisation. However, conflict of interest was, for the first time, raised at this meeting, as subsidies to countries operating from Central Europe may give them competitive advantage over existing community countries, thus creating antagonism and potential disharmony.

Central East European Privatisation Network (CEEPN)

CEEPN Secretariat
Titovea 104
61000 Ljubljana
Slovenia
Tel: 3861-346 361

A network formed by Bulgaria, Czechoslovakia, Hungary, Poland and Romania to support privatisation through information sharing, training and technical workshops.

The country profiles in this chapter are somewhat different from the subsequent chapters. They do not cover business etiquette and the subtle nuances of personal business transactions, as the business community is fragile and immature. What is attempted is a brief description of the current economic conditions for business development. In all cases, the lessons of civility and respect laid out in the following chapters should be put into practice, and a sound understanding of the struggle and the successes achieved by the country you wish to trade with should be sought. Make no less effort to facilitate a trading relationship with any of the Eastern European countries than you would with existing members of the EU, in fact, add flexibility, innovation and creativity to your approach. Most government bodies and private individuals will be delighted to receive your approaches, and generous with their time and energies. However, because of the transitional status of their economic infrastructures, making things happen may generally be slower than in other economies.

To enable businesspeople to keep in touch with the progress in these countries, a magazine called the *East European Reporter* is published bi-monthly, and is available in English from The Editor, Budapest 1015, Csalogany Utca 6-10.111.118, Hungary, or from The Economist Bookshop, London. Another source of information is the series of guides published by the DTI entitled 'Hints to Exporters'. These are excellent, if not always entirely up-to-date, and they publish one for each of the following countries except Albania. The World Aid Section of the DTI maintains a database, and can assist with trading and legislative information in preparation for visits to Central and Eastern Europe.

ALBANIA

The poorest, most isolated 'liberated' member of the Soviet bloc is in real trouble trying to adjust to its new-found freedoms. Totally ill-equipped to embark on a free market economic system, its political and social structures are unstable.

The country has a population of around three million, and although the first free elections took place in March 1991, the resulting split representation of the old Communist party and the new Urban Democratic party produced futile political polarisation. The country's crime rate has risen: thefts from shops increasing by over 300 per cent in 1991, and internal ethnic problems prevent a uniform national focus. So much so that both Italy and Greece have had to deal with huge exoduses of desperate people arriving from Albania.

In June 1990 private enterprises were allowed, but they are mainly small, family service businesses, and farmers selling extra food. Foreign investors are allowed to own companies, but not property. The country's industrial infrastructure is old, and it will be both time-consuming and expensive to reconstruct, partly as the workforce is ill-equipped both in tools and in education. Although 1991 saw a privatisation programme to encourage foreign investors, the attractiveness of a country whose industrial and agricultural production in 1991 was 55 per cent down on 1990 is limited. As a leading Albanian politician put it, 'the theories of Marx and Lenin have led to misery, poverty and despair'. Unfortunately, it is debatable whether the patient is fit enough for the free market remedy.

An unlikely place to start any business expansion into Central Europe.

Useful addresses

Chamber of Commerce of the People's Republic of Albania
Kruga Konferenca e Pezes 6
Tirana

BULGARIA

Bulgaria's break with Communism was anything but clean. Although in the most recent elections it is claimed that over two-thirds of the people voted against Communism, the Union of Democratic Forces still only won a marginal majority. The government formed, however, has pressed on hard with social, political and industrial reforms. The delay caused by political squabbling in implementing the radical reforms required by the country cannot hide the enthusiasm for change. The Prime Minister, Philip Dimitriov, when asked what he could offer private business replied with one word: 'opportunities'.

Bulgaria has started a robust and adventurous commercial restructuring programme. With help from the International Monetary Fund (IMF) and other agencies, it is building a solid capital market-place which will encourage commercial banking, foreign investment and political enterprise. The opening of the Stock Exchange in late 1991 is just one example of this. However, Bulgaria has as yet been unable to deliver much of its stated intentions, and it will take time for the Government to complete its basic privatisation legislation. Even when the passage of laws on commerce, foreign investment and competition has been completed, the country still has a long way to catch up with the 'triangle' countries, although it is probably closer than either Romania or Albania. However, some progress on trade agreements with the EU has been made.

Bulgarian business hours are similar to those in the UK, starting at 8.45 am through to 12.30 pm, and then 1.00 pm through to 5.30/6.00 pm. Like other European countries, shaking hands opens and closes each meeting, but be aware that a nod of the head sometimes means 'no' rather than 'yes'. Hospitality is generous, but wives will not usually be invited. English is probably the most important foreign language and it can be spoken in business without giving offence.

Useful addresses

Embassy of the Republic of Bulgaria
186–8 Queen's Gate
London SW7 5HL
Tel: 071-584 9400/9433

Bulgarian Industrial Association
134 Kakouzki Street
Sofia
Tel: 359 288 2501

National Tourism Office
1 Boulevard Vitosa
Sofia
Tel: 359 243331

European Documentation Centre
Bulgarian Academy of Sciences
Centre for European Studies
VI Dobromiv Huiz 7
Sofia
Tel: 359-2-44-14-96

Interpred Association
16 Bulgaro-Svetska Druzhba
Sofia 1057
Tel: 359-71-46-46-46

Bulgarian Chamber of Commerce
11a Stamvolustu Bouluevard
Sofia
Tel: 359-2-87-26-31/87-07-41

CZECH AND SLOVAK FEDERAL REPUBLIC

As a pre-War centre of cultural and economic world influence, the Czech and Slovak Federal Republic has retained its independent spirit, and is taking a leading role in the emergence of the new European order. The relatively smooth transition to a democratic state has done much to enhance the country's reputation.

The Czech and Slovak Federal Republic's workforce is relatively well-skilled, giving it an advantage over, and a market for its products and skills to, the old East as well as to the rest of the world. Having gained associate trading status with the EU, it is looking for full membership by the year 2000. However, risks and difficulties in doing business do exist:

- the economy is still volatile, proper tax legislation will not be introduced until 1993 and basic wages are still centrally determined;
- the federal/confederate status of the Czechs and the Slovaks is unresolved, even after the agreement in June 1991 to politically split; and
- the embryonic state of the commercial infrastructure could all cause short-term risk to investment, although increases to competitiveness should lead to longer-term benefits.

The Republic's government has gone a long way to encourage foreign trade, and major joint ventures have begun to emerge and succeed. Procter and Gamble purchased Rokana, a detergent manufacturer, and has plans to centralise all its detergent manufacturing through Rokana for the whole of its European markets. The financial infrastructure is fairly robust within the country, with merchant banks well established, a stock market active and consumers using credit cards. Privatisation has gone ahead with an innovative voucher system which allows individuals to hold shares which can be converted into company-specific ownership or a type of mutual fund.

The Czech government encourages foreign investment, giving tax incentives, no limit on the repatriation of trading profits and little restriction on the industries or the form of participation that foreign investors can make.

The Republic is rapidly taking its place again as a vibrant European member state and, with a population of over 15 million, has a potential appropriate to its historic status.

When dealing with Czechs or Slovaks, punctuality is important. The business hours are 8.00 am to 4.00 pm and, as in France, it is advisable to avoid a visit during the vacational months of July and August. The main foreign language is German and interpreters are recommended if you are not able to transact business in their native language or German.

Useful addresses

Embassy of the Czech and Slovak Federal Republic
25 Kensington Place Gardens
London W8 4QY
Tel: 071-229 1255

Czechoslovakian Chamber of Commerce
Argentinska 38
170 05
Prague 7
Tel: (422) 87 91 34

Czech Association of Entrepreneurs
Stavoměstské námĕsti 6
110 01 Prague 1
Tel: (422) 232 0752

National Information Centre
Havelkova 22
130 00 Prague 3
Tel: (422) 236 14 94-5

Agency for Foreign Investment of the Czech Republic Ministry for Economic Policy and Development
Konviktskà 5
110 00 Prague 3
Tel: (422) 22-67 51-54

European Reference Centre
Slovenska Technika Kniznica
Nam Slobody L19
81223 Bratislava

HUNGARY

The Hungarian government's move towards social and political liberation has been evolutionary rather than radical. Direct investment is encouraged, a long-term economic plan has been put in place and, with an economy which most resembles that of the West, its chances of success are good. Hungary offers a strong potential for development, and has a population of over eleven million. Like the other members of the 'triangle', it has associate membership of the EU, and has undertaken massive privatisation plans. The State Property Agency has been entrusted with converting state enterprises into private companies, with the aim of achieving this by the end of 1992. Private investment is encouraged, although a voucher system similar to that of Poland and the Czech and Slovak Federal Republic has not been introduced.

The financial infrastructure of Hungary is sophisticated, with a stock and commodity market as well as a substantial presence of European merchant banks. Politically, the country is as stable as any of the emerging European states, and has a good reputation in the international money community for the steps taken by the Hungarian National Bank to secure a free market economy within Hungary.

The Hungarians are friendly and hospitable. Social behaviour is more formal than in Britain, and people shake hands on every occasion. Business visiting cards are used extensively and business hours are similar to the Czech and Slovak Federal Republic. Hospitality can be generous! Business is usually conducted in Hungarian, and interpreters have previously been provided by the company but, where this is not done, they can be obtained from the Tourist Office.

Useful addresses

Embassy of the Republic of Hungary
35 Eaton Place
London SW1X 8BY
Tel: 071-235 4048/7191

Hungarian Chamber of Commerce
Kossuth Lajos ter 6–8
1055 Budapest
Tel: 36 1533 333

Hungarian Tourist Board
Dorolta V4
1051 Budapest
Tel: 36 1186 354

Hungarian Foreign Trade Bank
Szent Istuan ter 11
Budapest V
H-1821
Tel: 36 132 9360

State Property Agency
Vigado Utca 6
Budapest
Tel: 36 118 5044

Association of Entrepreneurs
Szunet ut 15
118 Budapest
Tel: 36 185 3377

European Reference Centre
College of Commerce, Hospitality and Tourism
Alkotany Utca 9–11
HV-1054 Budapest
Tel: 36 1 327 150

POLAND

Perhaps seen as the leading light in the liberalisation of the Eastern European economic system since the early days of recognition of Solidarity in September 1980 and the high profile of its president, Lech Walesa, transition to a free market has not been smooth. Sixty per cent of the Polish workforce are still in state-owned companies, and productivity in most industries is down on 1989. In fact, the World Bank has gone as far as to say Poland's reforms are at a crossroads. Indicative of the lack of hard decision-making is the absence of any major liquidation or bankruptcies since the initial moves towards privatisation in 1989. The whole privatisation process has taken longer than anticipated, and Poland has now sought outside advisors to help in this process on an industry-by-industry basis. For instance, Price Waterhouse is the advisor for the glass industry and Coopers & Lybrand has been appointed for car components.

The Polish people's involvement in privatisation has mainly been through a free voucher system based on shares in mutual funds run by foreign investment managers and consisting of the top 400 privatised companies. The political system is fragmented (29 different parties have seats in the Parliament) with a surprisingly early apathy in the democratic process with only 42 per cent of people voting in the 1991 elections. Criticism of both the government and the president's ability to transform the economy on free market lines has emerged through the press. However, Poland has the largest population and GNP of the Central and Eastern European countries, of approximately 38 million and US$140 billion respectively. It also has a workforce with a high standard of education and skills. Should Poland develop a free market economy and stabilise its political system, then the progress made in establishing a legislative and institutional framework to attract foreign investment should bear productive fruits.

Polish foreign business is usually conducted in English but, if not, interpreters can be arranged through the Tourist Office. Again, working hours are from about 8.30 am, often straight through until 4.00 pm, so don't be surprised if there is no meal break. Hospitality, when it arrives, is generous.

Useful addresses

Embassy of the Republic of Poland
47 Portland Place
London W1N 3AG
Tel: 071-580 4324

Polish Chamber of Foreign Trade
ul Trebacka 4
PO Box 361
00-950 Warsaw
Tel: 48 22 26 02 21

Polish Marketing Association
Navy Swiat 49
Room 401
00042
Warsaw
Tel: 48 276953

Central Statistical Office
Al Niepodleglosci 208
00925 Warsaw
Tel: 48 253 241

National Bank of Poland
ul Swelokiyska 11/12
00950 Warsaw
Tel: 48 200 321

Industry Ministry
ul Wspolna 4
00 926 Warsaw
Tel: 48 210 351

European Reference Centre
Institut au conjoncture et des Prix du commerce exterieure
Centre de L'éference sur les CE
ul Swelokrzyska 12
Pl - 00916 Warsaw
Tel: 48 694 4210

ROMANIA

Ironically, Romania has travelled the furthest towards the level of liberalisation and the embracing of market forces within its economy of all the 'triangle' countries. The irony is that the nationalism present in all Central and Eastern European countries attempting to escape from Communism is particularly virulent in Romania. The political instability of the country could lead outsiders to believe that Romania is happy to change its economic system, but its xenophobic relationship with the world, Europe and its own ethnic minorities causes the reality to be significantly different.

However, privatisation was legalised in June 1991, and with it a wide-ranging infrastructure to ensure 30 per cent of ownership of transferred Romanian state enterprises went to Romanians totally free. A banking system to support commercial trade, agencies to prepare companies for privatisation and a system to encourage trading and purchase (through auctions) of shares have been set up. Wide-ranging legislation is in place to encourage foreign investment and trade, with tax incentives on profits for reinvestment and assurances on the repatriation of profits. I would recommend a personal assessment of the spirit for international trade before any commercial activities. A number of European banks have offices in Bucharest, including Manufacturers Hanover Trust and Societe Generale, and these would be a sensible place to begin a commercial evaluation.

Romanians begin business early – at about 8.00 am, and work up to about 4.00 pm. English is as common a foreign language as French and German, and translators are usually available within State organisations or can be booked through the National Tourist Office. Hospitality is given and received with generosity, and small company mementos are well received.

Useful addresses

Embassy of Romania
4 Palace Green
London W8 4QD
Tel: 071-937 9666

Romanian Bank for Foreign Trade SA
22–4 Calea Victorici
Bucharest
Tel: 149190 147378

National Bank of Romania
25 Lipscani Street
Bucharest

Commercial Bank of Romania
14 Bulevardus Republicii
Bucharest

European Documentation Centre
Université de Bucharest
Faculté de Droit
Bdul M Kogalniceanu 64
Sector 5
Bucharest
Tel: 149190 154947

Post-Maastricht, the mechanisms for a single market have been put in place, but the convergence of national attitudes into a European psyche has been slow. In a recent *Financial Times* survey, over 77 per cent of the top European companies stated that they saw no benefit from the 1993 lowering of Europe's internal trade barriers. Indeed, while 50 per cent wanted easier access for Asia and Eastern Europe, some countries (France and Spain) wanted higher trade barriers. Britain, who was the least attracted to deepening Union integration, is the most sceptical regarding the competitive advantages of a single European currency. The question of whether Europe will remain competitive during the next ten years shows a split between the North and South, with the Northern countries showing a greater fear that Europe will slip behind. In another survey conducted amongst the general public in 1993, reaction to the single market was equivocal. Behind the results below seems to be a general feeling that others, rather than themselves, are more likely to benefit from the Union. The attitudes of both business and consumers show the daunting task faced by governments at the Maastricht review conference in 1996. The compromises struck to facilitate the signing of the Maastricht Treaty will be tested to the limit.

Table 7.1 For or Against the Maastricht Treaty

Country	% For	% Against	% Undecided
Belgium	45	18	37
Denmark	57	27	16
France	44	37	19
Greece	44	17	39
Germany	41	29	30
Ireland	62	17	21
Italy	41	10	49
Luxembourg	44	20	36
Netherlands	58	10	32
Portugal	30	20	50
Spain	38	20	42
UK	28	35	37
Average	41	42	37

The following pages are a country-by-country guide which, if they show anything, highlight the problem of considering Europe to be more than a legislative single market.

PART 2
A COUNTRY BY
COUNTRY GUIDE*

*In this edition the activities of member states to promote the advantages of the single market have been deleted, as the single market is now a reality.

8
BELGIUM

INTRODUCTION

Belgium is a country of two nations, or, more accurately, of one nation speaking two different languages: the North speak Dutch and the South speak French (except in the western Liege province, where there are German, French and protected Dutch-German speaking communities). An understanding of the differences is useful, as they can have a major impact on businesses which span the two areas. Nowhere else in Europe does one nation have two quite distinct ethnic and linguistic communities: the Germanic Dutch-speaking Flemish in the North and the Latin, French-speaking Walloons in the South. To complicate matters, Brussels is a largely French-speaking island situated 20 miles into Flemish territory.

For the Briton, the language division can be a positive advantage, as it creates a common communication channel: English. Its usefulness is based on its neutral status and it can be used in all regions of Belgium.

Central to the European concept of Brussels (the home of the EU Commission and a key community city) being the EU host capital, historically Belgium has generally looked towards its neighbours for trade. It was one of the founder members of the Community. The Belgian people do not regard their linguistic homelands in a separate way as, for instance, do the Scottish Nationalists in the UK or the Basques in Spain, they are proud of their monarchy and enjoy the sense of unity and national identity which it bestows.

Today, Belgium is mainly an industrialised nation. A close relationship is still maintained with Luxembourg, whose currency is tied to the Belgian franc. Class and education snobbery in Belgium is not usual; however, whatever beneficial transaction is done for one of the main language groups will have to be matched for the others.

MAKING THE APPOINTMENT

The meetings should be arranged initially by letter, which should be written in English unless you are sure of the language in use: Antwerpen Dutch, Mons French, etc. English is recommended if writing to a company in Brussels, but at all times bear in mind the delicacy of the situation.

A letter should be well written (particularly if it is in business French) and you should offer to provide an interpreter at a subsequent meeting. Badly-written letters are likely to be rejected immediately, although any attempt to communicate in Dutch rather than French is more appreciated in the South. A letter can be followed up within two weeks of sending. When following up the letter, however, do note that the Belgian postal service is not the fastest in Europe!

The secretarial role varies from region to region; generally, in the North, the secretary is more likely to hold the executive's diary and to act on his behalf. Be careful how you address the secretary as informality is only acceptable after an appropriate length of time.

THE MEETING

If the letter is written in English, there is no insistence on interpretation, but as mentioned before, to provide a French or Dutch speaker for the meeting would be appreciated. When attending a meeting, the European custom of hand-shaking will apply across both cultures. Small talk is reserved for generalities, and getting down to business will occur quite quickly. Coffee or tea will usually be served at the meeting.

Formality is still very much the norm on the first meetings, with the initial meeting conducted on surname terms. Only after the relationship has continued for several meetings is the use of first names likely. It is also important to be on time: if you are late, then your appointment is likely not to be honoured or will at least be restricted which is not a good start.

Family life is important to Belgians, and they set aside time for it. They will also visit their extended families regularly, as often as once a week.

Belgians see themselves as more efficient, more reliable and producing higher quality goods than most other countries. Belgians also believe themselves to be more hardworking and less friendly, at least at the beginning of a relationship. They are more cautious than, say, the Dutch.

ENTERTAINING

Business meals

Breakfast meetings are unusual in Belgium. Breakfast is taken at home; although early morning meetings are not uncommon, these would not involve having a meal.

The likelihood of a lunch invitation has little to do with your rapport and more to do with the focus of the business proposition and the point it has reached. Lunch will normally take between one and two hours, starting at noon. The person extending the invitation normally pays the bill. Eating out is customary in Belgium, so ask your host for the names of appropriate restaurants if you are extending the invitation.

Dinner invitations are usually longer and less frequent than lunch. If the invitation is for dinner at the person's home then it certainly shows a progression in the relationship since Belgian people do tend to separate home from business life.

If you are invited home, you should bring flowers with you; do not bring any form of drink. When you meet the lady of the house, shake hands; cheek kissing only occurs once greater familiarity is achieved.

Belgians are famed for their hospitality, so be forewarned. If a Belgian decides to take you out on the town, it will be a long and expensive business. It is best to decline until the negotiations are concluded, as it is very difficult to match practised Belgians at socialising, particularly if a meeting is scheduled for the following day!

In all dealings with Belgians, be prepared for the best of everything; if you are entertained, particularly at home, you will be utterly spoiled.

Subjects for social discussion

When making small talk, bear in mind that the Belgians set great store by their homes, the same applies to the town or city in which they live. Remarks about the town or city if made in positive statements are helpful, as are comments on family life. Whatever else you discuss, never mention the language division as this is a very delicate topic.

Business hospitality

Other than in the cultural centres of Belgium, opportunities for business hospitality are limited. However, the Belgians are unlikely to commit company marketing budgets to corporate hospitality. One-to-one meetings, perhaps an invitation to an important sports event, are more likely to be offered, based on your host's personal interests.

Gifts

Gifts should be restricted to the functional, logoed business object. Extravagant gifts will be rejected.

Dress

It is very important to dress well and stylishly. Men should wear dark suits, shirts and ties – the tie should remain on in all circumstances. For women, trousers are usually unacceptable, as are short skirts; stockings or tights are always worn, even in summer.

WOMEN IN BUSINESS

In Belgium, the role of women is changing rapidly. They are not, however, employed in the most senior jobs in the country. Belgium has the highest female unemployment percentage in Europe, but its general rate is on par with the rest of the Community.

WORKING HOURS AND PUBLIC HOLIDAYS

The usual working day starts at 8.00 or 8.30 am, lunch is taken between 12.00 and 1.00 pm, and the day finishes around 6.00 pm. The normal holiday entitlement is four weeks, split into two two-week holidays. Summer holidays fall in with school holidays, which are taken during July and August. Unlike the UK, Christmas, New Year and Easter are restricted to the basic holidays plus a day or two.

1st January	(New Year's Day)
1st May	(Labour Day)
21st July	(National Day)
15th August	(Assumption)
1st November	(All Saint's Day)
11th November	(Armistice Day)
25th December	(Christmas Day)

In addition there are three movable days, including Easter.

LETTER-WRITING

For letter-writing, see the appropriate sections on France, the Netherlands and the UK, pages 113, 181 and 217. If in doubt about which language to use you should opt to write in English.

MARKETING

The marketing spend in Belgium remained fairly constant in line with media inflation until recently, when a small increase occurred. The country's bilingual nature has resulted in a split in level of infrastructure which supports Belgian-built agencies. Belgium, therefore, has a large number of agencies of American origin. Another reason for the increase is, because of its culture and communication channels, Belgium provides an ideal testing ground for European campaigns. The major changes in marketing spends are an increase in below-the-line activity and a greater investment in direct marketing.

Socio-economically, the country is split into four groups:

Table 8.1   Socio-economic grading in Belgium

	%
A	3
B	16
C1	46
C2	15
Other	20

Source CIM

The media spend, in Belgian francs, is spread in the following way:

Table 8.2   Media spend in Belgium

	%
Newspapers	24
Freesheets	9
Consumer magazines	33
Television	16
Radio	2
Cinema	1
Outdoor, transport	15

Source AAS/CACP

The spend rankings by key categories are:

Table 8.3   Spend categories in Belgium

(1)	Automotive
(2)	Department stores
(3)	Finance
(4)	Clothing, shoes
(5)	Alcohol, wines, beer
(6)	Cosmetics, hair-care

Source AAS

Media

There are no special advertising taxes. VAT is levied at 19 per cent. Advertising is not ᴀllowed on national state-owned TV and radio channels, except 'non-commercial' generic informa-tion-style advertisements and public service announcements. Alcohol advertising is not allowed on TV or radio. Certain restrictions exist on outdoor advertising. Tobacco advertising is not allowed on TV or radio and in the cinema only basic information is allowed, such as the pack and the price; it must also carry a health warning. Restrictions on advertising tobacco outdoors include a restriction on the size of the poster-billboard to no more than $16m^2$. Press advertisements for tobacco are restricted to no more than half a page per brand in newspapers and one page in magazines. There are severe restrictions on most pharmaceutical advertising. For further information contact: Jury d'Ethique Publicitaire, Rue des Colonies 54, PO Box 13, 1000 Brussels (Tel: +32 2 219 06 62).

CONSUMER PREFERENCES/DIFFERENCES

Household spend

The Belgians take great pride in their homes. As such it is not surprising to find that they spend a considerable amount of money on purchases for their home.

Belgium ranks third in consumer spend on home furnishings and is at the top of the spend category for the whole range of household electrical appliances. The consumer spend on the latter could be considered essential to their way of life as opposed to a consumer preference.

Because of the work pattern in Belgium (and the same

applies for Denmark), basic household appliances, which ease the workload at home, can be found in 90 per cent of all households. These appliances include washing machines, fridges and vacuum cleaners. For example, food processors sales in Belgium are the highest in Europe.

The Belgians' love of all things beautiful in their home by no means stops at the convenience or essential level. In the EC spend on items such as tableware and cutlery Belgium again tops the list. Another high area of consumer spend is in the level of board games. Belgium ranks close to the top of the sales in the market penetration of home computers. Although, interestingly, ownership of video machines is one of the lowest in the EU.

The population in Belgium is about 10 million and, although smaller in comparison to the population of France or Germany, the consumer demand represents a good target market for manufacturers of home-related appliances.

The statistical breakdown of household spend on domestic goods and services is as follows:

Table 8.4   Belgian household spend

Items	%
Furniture (including carpets and other floor coverings)	29
White goods	15
Furnishings	10
Tableware and utensils	17*
Domestic and other household services	29

Source Eurostat/Mintel
*Note** the highest spend in EU.

Financial awareness

Most major banks have a presence in Belgium, and bank services are well used, for example, 71 per cent of Belgiums have a bank account compared to the UK figure where only 45 per cent of the populace have a bank account (although this figure has shown a marked increase over the last 10 years). Credit cards are not considered essential, however, with only 5 per cent of the population holding a card. Building societies are not used as much as banks with only 17 per cent of the population holding accounts.

Food spend

The introduction of hypermarkets is well accepted with 75 per cent of people shopping there.

In meat consumption, the Belgians' preference is for pork and they spend very little on mutton, lamb or goat. Fish on the other hand, is regularly consumed.

The Belgians are the third largest consumer of meat per capita in the European Union. To wash this down Belgians drink more mineral water than anywhere else in Europe and drink more beer per capita than the English!

General consumer spend

Foreign designed clothes rank high on Belgian preferences in clothing. They clearly prefer to buy clothes from foreign designers rather than their own industry. But compared to their European partners, the Belgians do not spend a great deal on clothes; indeed, they spend more on beer than they do on clothes!

When selecting a car or consumer durables Belgians will buy products made in their country rather than purchase foreign-made items.

Political trends

Although the green issues put forward by the Ecologist Party showed the Belgians have a keen interest in their environment, the Socialist Party just 'pipped' the Christian Democrats gaining eight seats as opposed to seven.

Voter awareness of issues is high with a 93 per cent turnout of voters. Belgium has 24 Euro seats.

ESTABLISHING A BUSINESS

Prior authorisation is only required for certain types of business; for example, transport, insurance and banking.

Most foreigners who do business in Belgium set up a limited company, either private or public. Both types of company are governed by the same 'company laws'; accordingly, the major differences being in the size of capital and the nature of shares. No special consents are needed, except in certain closely defined activities relating to specific products. Statutory documents must be deposited with the Belgian equivalent of Britain's Companies House system. Each year 5 per cent of each company's profit must be put into a legal reserve until the reserve equals 10 per cent of the issued capital. This reserve may not be distributed, but there is no other limitation on the repatriation of profits.

Foreign companies can operate in Belgium through a subsidiary, incorporated under Belgian law, or through a Belgian branch of a company. The following types of company may be used although a corporation, *Naamloze Vennotschap (NV)* or Société Anonyme SA, is most common.

- corporation (SA–NV);
- private limited company (SPRL–BVBA);
- general partnership (SNC–VOF);
- limited partnership (SCS–VEG);
- partnership limited by shares (SCA–VGA);
- societé cooperative (S Coop-Coop V).

The minimum legal capital for a SPRL–BVBA is BF 750,000 and for a SA–NV, BF 1,250,000. Both are governed by the same legal requirements, but only a SA–NV can be listed on the Stock Exchange. Shares in a SPRL–BVBA are represented by 'parts sociales'.

A subsidiary set up as a Belgian company is required to comply with Belgian company law, whether or not the shareholders are foreign nationals or companies. Company directors may be foreign nationals. There is no legal requirement that a Belgian national should own part of the share capital.

Every corporation must file its articles of incorporation, the names of its directors and statutory auditors, and its annual financial statements at the appropriate Register of Commerce.

Foreign companies may set up branches in Belgium. Branches are governed by the same regulations as Belgian companies as regards management and operations in Belgium; they must appoint local representatives and register certain documents.

Foreign companies wishing their Belgian branch to engage in trade or manufacture are required to file a certified copy of the parent company's articles of incorporation together with any amendments with the Trade Register of Commerce. A statement by the parent company's board authorising the establishment of the branch and the delegation of powers to the branch management, and the name and address of its official representative in Belgium, should also be filed.

The branch must also register with the Register of Commerce where it is located, obtain a registration number and keep appropriate legal and accounting records.

Management structure

A SPRL–BVBA is managed by one or more directors, who do not have to be holders of 'parts sociales' or company shares. They are elected by the shareholders. Once elected they are allowed to run the company in whichever way they see fit, inside or outside the objects of the company's articles of incorporation. They have to prepare an annual inventory, accounts and management report for the shareholders.

In a SA–NV, the company is managed by at least three directors, appointed at a general meeting. They have the ability to delegate the daily management of the company, but are liable to third parties for transgression.

Since 1986, all companies meetings the following criteria have to appoint a statutory auditor:

- annual turnover of BF 145,000,000;
- balance sheet totals of BF 70,000,000;
- annual average of 50 persons employed.

In a SA–NV company or SPRL–BVBA, if there are more than 100 employees, a workers' council of equal numbers of employer and employee representatives must be set up. A meeting must be convened at least once a month to review working conditions and the progress of the company. It is seen as a co-operative association.

USEFUL ADDRESSES

Sources of information and help

Belgo-Luxembourg Chamber of Commerce in Great Britain Inc
6 John Street
London WC1N 2ES
Tel: 071-831 3508
Fax: 071-831 9151

British Chamber of Commerce for Belgium and Luxembourg
30 Rue Joseph II
B-1040 Brussels
Tel: (+32) 02 2190 788
Tlx: 64580 BRICOM B

Research sources

Federation of Belgian Market Research Institutes
PO Box 16
1040 Brussels
Tel: (+32) 02 219 1100

Aspemar SA, (full market research service)
Avenue des Arts 2
Boite 16
B-1040 Brussels
Tel: (+32) 02 2191100
Tlx: 65409 ASMAR B

Addresses for advertisers

Jury d'Ethique Publicitaire
Rue des Colonies 54, (details of advertising restrictions)
PO Box 13
1000 Brussels
Tel: (+32) 02 2190662

Association des Grandes Enterprises de Distribution, (major
retailers representative body)
Rue de la Science 3
B-1040 Brussels
Tel: (+32) 02 5373060

Belgian Association of Advertising Agencies
28 Rue du Barbeau
1160 Brussels
Tel: (+32) 02 673 2387

Chambers of Commerce

Brussels
Avenue–Louise 580
1050 Brussels
Tel: (+32) 02 648 5002

Antwerp
Markgravestraat 12
Antwerp
Tel: (+32) 03 232 2219

Principal Euro Info Centres

Euro Info Centre
Avenue Sergent Vrithoff 2
B-5000 Namur
Tel: (+ 32) 81 73 52 09

Euro Info Centre
Markgravestraat 12
B-2000 Antwerpen
Tel: (+ 32) 03 233 7658

9
DENMARK

INTRODUCTION

Denmark, despite its reputation as the land of fairy tales and make-believe villages, is in reality a sophisticated nation whose economic centre has shifted away from agriculture to service and light industries. It has a flexible manufacturing base, the entrepreneurial spirit of which is thriving.

Denmark is a liberal-minded, tolerant, compact nation with a low crime rate, a deep sense of social welfare and strong cooperative links with immediate neighbours. Danes have a great sense of humour and are much more interested in the good life than in power and politics. They also react with stubborn resistance to outside pressure.

A strong entrepreneurial spirit is evident within the business structure, and there is a constant spin-off from larger firms into smaller companies. More than half of all industrial jobs are in companies with under 200 staff.

MAKING THE APPOINTMENT

Beginning a business relationship with a Danish company requires a formal approach. It is best to write the initial letter in English and ensure that it states the purpose and the goals of the proposed meeting. The Danish attitude to language is similar to the Dutch in that they recognise the smallness of their population (and land mass) in relation to the rest of Europe and consequently know that they must adapt to speaking other languages. Even so, it would be appreciated by your Danish counterparts to offer to provide an interpreter, particularly if you are dealing with one of the smaller, family-owned companies, the head of which may not be used to negotiating in a foreign language.

The secretarial role is a well-defined one and, as in most Northern European countries, the secretary plays a significant part in the organised business life of your Danish counterpart. You may assume that she is an extension of the individual to whom you wish to speak.

THE MEETING

The Danes' one obsession is with punctuality, so do make sure you arrive on time for appointments, whether business or social. If you know you will be more than a few minutes late, ring. Once at the meeting, small talk is limited. Be prepared for hardheaded, direct discussions and have all the facts at your fingertips.

The Danish language reflects, as do French and German, the closeness or formality of a relationship. When discussion is in English, formality is always best, but will be relaxed very quickly, given the potential for a good rapport, particularly if your business contact is fairly young.

Danes do not go in for lengthy haggling, and they expect that your proposition will be thoroughly worked out before you present it to them. If they are going to do business with you, it is because they have identified you as an expert in your market, and they will expect the proposition to reflect that. The Danes are likely to walk away from a poorly-put business proposition, even when they know (from past experience or previous introduction) that you have a worthwhile product, so it is important to be thorough and precise.

Their high standard of living should make the Danes a consumer market. They are aware of this, and expect imported products to be of the highest quality in order to compete with their home-produced goods.

The 'moralistic', rather dull, image of the Danes may be an accurate prejudice so far as business meetings are concerned, but the subsequent relationship is usually very far from being dull; indeed it will probably prove to be quite the opposite. The Danes' reputation for admirable organisation should not be confused with restrictiveness and limitations.

ENTERTAINING

Business meals

The Danish breakfast, being a substantial meal (cheese, meats, eggs, cake, bread and gallons of coffee), is an opportunity for business meetings. The Danes begin work between 8.00 and 8.30 am and finish between 4.00 and 5.00 pm. Only half an hour is normally taken for lunch, and the British and Spanish lunch culture is certainly not apparent in Denmark. Business lunches do occur, but more likely (perhaps because of the size of breakfast) is the offer of a business dinner.

Dinner may be taken at your host's home or at a restaurant. It is unlikely that being invited home will be of any significance to your business transaction. Your business counterpart's partner is likely to attend, even if you dine at a restaurant.

Should you be invited home, then flowers are the most appropriate gift for the hostess. The bouquet should be produced by a florist, and presented wrapped, to the hostess. It is also important to telephone and thank her the following day. A gift of whisky or brandy (*not wine*) is considered appropriate for the host.

Subjects for social discussion

It is as irritating to the Danes to be confused with other Scandinavian countries as it is for the Scots to be referred to as English or for that matter for the French-speaking Belgians to be mistaken for French nationals. An understanding of Danish geography, industrial infrastructure, history and major businesses will create a good impression: for example, in literature, Hans Christian Andersen and Karen Blixen; in science, Professor Bohr; in business, the major international companies of Bang and Olufsen, Lego and Danfoss. If you can also differentiate between Sweden, Norway and Finland, your acceptability will be enhanced.

Avoid discussions about the German occupation during the Second World War; discussions on the family, the house and non-controversial subjects are suitable topics. An appreciation of the high quality of Danish design and of their food would also be well received.

Business hospitality

Business hospitality is not formalised in the same manner as it is in the UK. The type of hospitality offered will be moulded to the interpersonal relationship. No lavish corporate entertainment industry exists.

Gifts

These are usually restricted to company pens, ashtrays, etc. It is important only to give such items if they are deemed to be stylish. The low standard of design incorporated in such items produced by many companies worldwide will do nothing to enhance your relationship or business presentation.

Dress

Business dress is less formal than in other countries in the EU, for example, in the UK and Germany. Blazers, suits and sweatshirts are all acceptable modes of dress for the Danish businessperson. Do not, however, assume such informality yourself, at least initially. A conservatively-styled suit, in a dark colour, with an appropriate tie and black shoes would be expected; save your jeans for sightseeing!

WOMEN IN BUSINESS

The high cost of living in Denmark has perhaps played an important role in introducing women into business life than previously admitted. It is quite common for both spouses to work away from home, and it then goes as a rule that the workload associated with cooking, childcare and cleaning is shared. In this environment, male dominance in business has been more quickly eroded than in most Northern European country members of the EU; of the number of applications for the Danish police force, 40 per cent of those received are from women. The Danes also have female tank crews.

WORKING HOURS AND PUBLIC HOLIDAYS

The Danes, as already mentioned, begin work fairly early in the day and finish after about eight hours. They take five weeks' holiday a year, of which three will usually be taken during July, as school holidays start in June and finish at the beginning of August. Christmas and Easter holidays are shorter than in the UK.

The major public holidays are:

1st January	(New Year's Day)
1st May	(Labour Day, afternoon)
5th June	(Constitution Day, afternoon)
25th/26th December	(Christmas Day)

There are six other movable public holidays, including Easter.

LETTER-WRITING

The envelope

English	Danish
Mr	Hr (forename[a], surname)
Mrs	Fru (forename, surname), or
Fr	(forename, surname)
Miss Frk	(forename, surname), or
Fr	(forename, surname)

Salutation

Danish	Letter written in: English
Kære Hr (surname)	Dear Mr (surname), or
	Dear Hr (surname)
Kære Fr (surname)	Dear Mrs (surname), or
	Dear Fr (surname)
Kære Fr (surname)	Dear Miss (surname), or
	Dear Fr (surname)
Not used	Dear Sir, Madam
Closing	
Individual med venlig hilsen	Yours sincerely
Company med venlig hilsen	Yours faithfully

Note
[a] The full forenames should always be written. It is usual practice to write initially to the department of the firm or organisation, not to an individual.

MARKETING

Commercial TV, cable TV and radio are the growth areas in advertising. Advertising as a whole in Denmark is affected to a greater extent by economic cycles than it is in most other European countries. However, the new media opportunities, combined with increased competition and squeezed margins, will eventually result in strong, high-profile agencies which will get stronger. The growth in the industry, if it occurs, is likely to be in the public and semi-public sectors: Post, Giro, Telecom and railways.

The Danish consumer is not standardised into groups by socio-economic classifications, so for marketing purposes one or more criteria such as income, housing, age and geographic location can be used.

The advertising spend is split as shown in Table 9.1.

Television advertising became available for the first time on 1 October 1988.

The spend rankings by key categories are shown in Table 9.2.

Table 9.1   Advertising spend in Denmark

	%
Newspapers	32
(Copenhagen	15)
Magazines	8
Freesheets	7
Cinema	1
Outdoor	2
Direct response	50

Source Danske Reklambureauers Brancheforening (DRB)

Table 9.2   Danish consumer spend

(1) Cars
(2) Department stores
(3) Financial
(4) EDP equipment
(5) Magazines
(6) Beer
(7) Non-alcoholic
    beverages

Source Gallup Markedsanalyse

Media

There is no special advertising tax. VAT is charged at 22 per cent. There are press restrictions on advertisements for alcoholic beverages, pharmaceutical products, tobacco and lottery promotions. New instructions have been issued by the

Minister of Culture and Communications concerning the content of advertisements on the new television channel. Among other things, the advertising of alcoholic beverages containing more than 2.25 per cent alcohol is banned. Also banned are tobacco products, medicines and political, religious and economist interest groups such as business associations and unions. A special set of rules concerning advertising to children and the use of children as models has been issued. For further information contact: Consumer Ombudsman, Bredgaede 31, Copenhagen 1260 (Tel: (+45) 1 138711).

CONSUMER PREFERENCES/DIFFERENCES

Household spend

The Danes can be regarded as the perfectionists of the EU. They insist upon stylish, well-made products; they are suspicious of products from other nations.

The Danes spend a considerable amount of money on home furnishings and electrical appliances. Perhaps because both partners work, these 'preferences' can almost be classed as essentials.

Like the Germans, the Danes prefer clear, bright definitions of colour in any article they buy.

Financial awareness

Denmark is an expensive country to live in compared to its fellow countries in the EU.

The bank system in Denmark is a sophisticated one, on par with the rest of Northern Europe.

Financial products, as known in the UK, are gradually becoming known, although there is some consumer resistance.

Food spend

All pork products are favourites. Fish is second on the Danes' list of preferences.

Consumption of other staple food products is average as is beer, wine and spirits.

General consumer spend

Denmark's population is circa six million, but despite this, the consumer spend is strong. The criterion when selecting goods has to be quality above all else.

Political trends

In Denmark, as in the UK, the loser in the Euro election was the Conservative Party. Out of a total of 16 Euro seats the Conservatives' total was reduced from four to two.

Voter apathy is not quite as pronounced as in the UK, with Denmark second from the bottom of the turnout table with 46 per cent.

ESTABLISHING A BUSINESS

Danish branches of foreign companies and all Danish companies must be registered in the Register of Companies (*Aktieselskabs-Registeret*). Other enterprises that carry on a trade or business must be registered in the Register of Commerce (*Handels-registeret*). However, sole traders are not obliged to register. Licences to trade are not required.

The two main types of company are private (*Anpartsselskab*, or ApS) and public (Aktieselskab, or A/S). Both are limited liability companies.

New businesses with an obligation to deduct tax from workers' or employees' pay must also register with the Central Tax Assessment Office (*Statsskattedirektoratet*) and businesses which are subject to value added tax (VAT) must also register with the VAT authorities. Social insurance registration is automatic following the notification to the Central Tax Assessment Office. There is no requirement to belong to any Chamber of Commerce or trade association.

The construction drawings for the erection or alteration of any building must be approved by the technical department of the municipality concerned.

No special rules apply to borrowing money within Denmark by Danish enterprises owned by non-residents.

Management structure

Every public limited company must have a Board of Directors (*bestyrelse*), consisting of at least three members. Substitutes or alternatives for individual directors may be appointed.

The Board of Directors must appoint a manager or board of managers (*direktion*). The managers are responsible for the day-to-day operations of the company, the Board of Directors being responsible for supervising the managers, laying down general policy making decisions on unusual transactions. All the managers, and at least half of the directors, must reside in Denmark (whatever their nationality) or be EU nationals resident in other EU member states. (The Ministry of Industry can, however, grant exemptions from this rule in certain circumstances.)

Members of the board of managers may serve on the Board of Directors but must always constitute a minority on that board. Corporate bodies cannot be appointed as either directors or managers.

If the articles of association so provide, the shareholders may elect a board of representatives (repraesentatskab) whose function is to supervise the directors and managers, but in practice such a board is rarely appointed.

In companies with an average of at least 35 employees (including hourly-paid workers) over the last three years, the employees are entitled, if they so wish, to elect to the board at least two further directors or half the number of directors elected by the shareholders (rounded up, if necessary, to the nearest whole figure), whichever is greater. In any company in which the employees exercise their entitlement, therefore, the minimum size of the Board of Directors is five. In addition, any group of companies (as defined by Companies Law) that has had an average of at least 35 employees over the last three years must, according to special rules, allow its employees to elect representatives to the Board of Directors of the parent company, if they so desire.

Works councils (samarbejdsudvalg), made up of equal numbers of representatives of management and labour, may be established in enterprises with at least 30 employees, if either the employer or more than 50 per cent of the employees so require. Rules as to works councils are usually laid down in collective agreements; although only members of employers' associations that are parties to those agreements are obliged to follow these rules, in practice all employers concerned do so. Works councils do not have any management powers or rights of veto over directors' or managers' decisions; they are principally used to communicate with and inform the employees. Individual councils' rules can stipulate the particular circumstances in which employees must be informed.

USEFUL ADDRESSES

Sources of information and help

British Import Union
Borsbygningen
DK-1217 Copenhagen K
Tel: (+45) 1 136349

Research sources

Institute for Media and Market Research in Scandinavia
1114 Copenhagen
Tel: (+45) 42 480800

Gallup Markedanalyse (part of Gallup organisation)
Gamnel Vartov Vej 6
DK-2900 Hellerup
Copenhagen
Tel: (+45) 1 298800
Tlx: 15180 GALLUP DK

Vilstrup Research (qualitative and quantitative
   research)
Godthabsvej 187
DK-2720 Copenhagen Vanlose
Tel: (+45) 1 866677
Tlx: 22988

Addresses for advertisers

Consumer Ombudsman (details of advertising
   legislation)
Bredgage 31
Copenhagen 1260
Tel: (+45) 1 138711

Danske Reklamebureaurers (Association of
   Danish Advertising Agencies)
Branchforening
Snaregade 12
1205 Copenhagen K
Tel: (+45) 1 134444

Chambers of Commerce

Copenhagen   Børsen (Stock Exchange)
                      1217 Copenhagen K
                      Tel: (+45) 339 12323

Principal Euro Info Centres

EF-Radgivnigskontoret for Fyn
Noorregade 51
DK-5000
Denmark
Tel: (+45) 9 146030

EF-Radgivnigskontoret
Haselgaardsvaenget 18–20
DK-8210 Arlins
Denmark
Tel: (+45) 625 0318

10
FRANCE

INTRODUCTION

French chauvinism is perhaps the overwhelming attribute of French business life. Some have likened it to arrogance based upon a long-past era when the French and the use of the French language were the centre of the diplomatic world. Today, you are at a distinct disadvantage in negotiations if one of your team does not speak good business French, for that is the language in which business will be conducted if the meeting is in France.

The French lifestyle is also changing. The Paris-based executive is much more of a Eurocrat, taking shorter lunchtimes and focusing more on the business goal. Staying late at the office is almost a status symbol, such status symbols being very important to the French. French business still has a strong affinity to the old money business families and great respect is also shown to the new breed of financiers who control, through holding companies, large sections of the business scene. A privatisation programme had begun, but was stopped due to the world stock market crash of 1987. The Paris scene is particularly rigid and formal, but on the Mediterranean coast and in the Midi people tend to be more accessible and more vague about timekeeping.

Snobbery in education is as significant in France as it is in the UK; being part of the *Grands Corps de l'Etat*. These are graduates of the *Grandes Ecoles* (usually *Ecole Polytechnique* or *Ecole Nationale d'Administration*). This backs up the marked class division that still exists, based more on background than on wealth. Only 13 per cent of university and college students come from working-class families.

In all business transactions with the French, it is best to remain formal and conservative. Do not be surprised by initial negative reactions to new ideas, and do not expect any snap decisions. A Frenchman is complimented by your respect for his nation and his culture (a good appreciation of his food and wine is also well received). He is hard in negotiations, expecting everything from courtesy to concession from his partner. These requirements are not necessarily matched by himself: a French negotiator who will speak in English is very much in need of the deal!

MAKING THE APPOINTMENT

The role of a secretary, for many French executives, is little more than that of a typist. Many senior executives still open their own post and keep their diaries, so what may seem like unco-operative behaviour from a secretary may simply be lack of knowledge. It is not unknown for letters to go unacknowledged for weeks because the boss is out of the office. However, a secretary can be an important influence in securing appointments, and it is worth developing a rapport, if you can.

French business is conducted very formally, and an initial interview is best requested in writing, and before the suggested date. The letter must conform to the best in business French. A poorly-constructed letter will lose impact or be totally disregarded. Address the letter to the head of the firm. Seek an initial meeting with the President/Directeur General, and send your most senior person to the meeting. Older people, in particular, like being called by their titles and if someone has several it is best to address him by the one he feels is most important, even if it is historic to his current job. Some managers do seem to think it increases their prestige to wait until very close to the appointment before replying. Be on time and well prepared for the meeting; they will expect you to be even if they are not themselves.

Initial contacts and more complex discussions usually take place in the firm's offices with experts and advisors present. Always shake hands when entering a meeting with all those present and those joining the meeting, and do the same on leaving. Do not expect refreshment during the meeting; this is not the custom. It is hard to over-stress the pride the French have in their achievements, whether it be sporting or economic. An awareness, and even appreciation, will be well received. Small talk, however, is limited in business meetings, which should be conducted in French. To assume that English (or any other language) will be spoken, even if you have had initial contact outside France in a business setting or social contacts within France and spoken English, will be to assume incorrectly as this will not be the case at the meeting. If you, or a member of your team, is not fluent then the meeting might just as well be cancelled. It is not unusual for the French businessman or official in such circumstances to stand and leave the meeting.

THE MEETING

Although younger people are more informal, the French still set great store by formal courtesies, titles and the right dress. It is safer to address your business partner as monsieur or madame, and to let the French set the pace.

Because of the legalistic nature of the French, every deal will tend to be drawn up in meticulous detail. Once the document is signed, however, it may be treated with a great deal of ambivalence. They will hold you to every letter of an agreement, while trying to find ways around it to suit themselves. The French have two kinds of rules: the written and the ones for actual use. Subtle tactics and good presentations are very important. Be well prepared, with good, solid, rational arguments and show commitment and enthusiasm. The French style of negotiations can include the switch of tactics to turn any negotiator on to the defensive even when responding to a French proposal. Once the deal is done, it will be hard work keeping to the terms. If you in any way do not match your commitment then you are likely to be sued. If they do not, look very carefully at the wording of the deal. It is always important to take contact notes of any business meeting and ensure acceptance of any decisions in writing and in detail.

Even if you have managed to develop a friendly rapport with your business partner, do not be surprised by the formality of his business letters. In France, anything put in writing is a serious business!

ENTERTAINING

Business meals
The breakfast meeting is fast establishing its place in the businesspersons' diary. Breakfast may be held in an hotel, a firm's executive dining room, or even a café. The meal will be more substantial than is usual for a normal French breakfast.

France is renowned for its cuisine and its lavish restaurant lunches. Business lunches can take up to three hours and will usually be very relaxed functions. Business is unlikely (naturally) to be discussed until the coffee stage, although to raise it earlier may be acceptable. Whoever issues the invitation should pay the bill, and it is quite acceptable for you to issue the invitation. However, remember that the French have a high regard for good food, so it might be appropriate to ask your guest to select the venue. It is likely to be expensive.

There is a movement away from the extended lunch, which is only likely to occur on occasions of success and celebration. In day-to-day relations, a quick brasserie lunch is common.

There is no special significance attached to being invited to dinner (unless it is to your host's home), which is fairly common in the provinces. Sometimes the host will bring his wife, but don't suggest it unless you have already met. If you should be invited to someone's home, you should follow the accepted niceties of not talking business until the coffee and brandy arrive, and not smoking before the cheese. As gifts, choose flowers or good chocolates for the hostess and malt whisky or cognac for the host – never wine!

The French are quite an hospitable race once you have passed their French admiration tests. Business entertaining may be cultural or sporting and should not be turned down. If you are invited away for the weekend, do make every effort to attend.

To conclude, the French will hold you strictly to the deal while it suits them, and breach it when it does not. Examine contracts very carefully as they can, and often do, lead to acrimonious relationships. Enter relationships on a long-term basis, for the short-term business deals will be difficult to achieve but, if you are successful in the longer term, the association could lead to a very good and profitable relationship.

Subjects for social discussion

Until fairly recently, it would have been quite unacceptable to talk about the cost of living or the size of your salary (although you might have been surprised at the openness of discussion about extra-marital relationships). French society has, however, become much more consumer-oriented of late, and people are more often judged by their success in business than they were in the past. French introversion should be respected; however, complimentary comments on their culture and wine would be well received.

Business hospitality

Grand hospitality at sponsored events does not occur as it does in the UK. Invitations may be given to the opera, a concert or to society horse race meetings.

Gifts

Gifts from the company such as a pen or diary with the company logo are acceptable. Very expensive gifts may cause offence.

Dress

Style is important to the French, thus dress should be smart, erring on the side of conservatism. Men will almost always wear a suit and tie, and women smart, chic, classic clothes. Even in hot weather, you would not be expected to shed your jacket and tie if your French host retains his. Dark suits are appropriate in Paris throughout the year, with lighter suits being acceptable in the summer.

WOMEN IN BUSINESS

France has accepted the role of female executives as well as any European country. In commerce, women hold senior, middle and junior management positions. In industry, however, some prejudice still exists. Women are expected to retain their femininity, even as successful businesspeople in 'a man's world'.

WORKING HOURS AND PUBLIC HOLIDAYS

The Parisians, in particular, work long hours, starting in their offices as early as 8.30 am and finishing at 8.00 in the evening. The French executive feels he deserves to take his weekend and holidays seriously: they should not be disturbed. Holidays are long – four to five weeks in summer and two weeks in winter. Because of these holidays, business usually stops from about mid-July to early September.

The main public holidays are:

1st January	(New Year's Day)
1st May	(Labour Day)
8th May	(Victory Day)
14th July	(Bastille Day)
15th August	(Assumption)
1st November	(All Saints' Day)
11th November	(Armistice Day)
25th December	(Christmas Day)

There are, in addition, three movable days, including Easter.

LETTER-WRITING

The envelope

French	English
Monsieur (first forename[a], surname)	Mr
Madame (first forename, surname)	Mrs
Mademoiselle (first forename, surname)	Miss

	Letter written in:
French	English
Monsieur[b] or if known Cher Monsieur	Dear Mr (surname)
	Dear Monsieur (surname)
Madame, or if known Chère Madame	Dear Mrs (surname) Madame
	Dear Madame (surname)
Mademoiselle	Dear Miss (surname)
	Dear Mademoiselle (surname)
Monsieur, Madame	Dear Sir, Dear Madam
Closing	
Individual Je vous prie d'agréer, (monsieur) l'expression de mes sentiments distingués	Yours sincerely
Company Je vous prie d'agréer, messieurs, l'expression de mes/nos sentiments distingués	Yours faithfully

Notes

[a] Initials are only used if the first name is not known. Except at senior level, it is normal to write to the particular department concerned, and not to the individual.

[b] If the letter is written in French, the surname is always omitted in the salutation.

MARKETING

The economic environment of France is stabilising, while expenditure is rising. Total expenditure on advertising is rising at over twice that of household expenditure. Media advertising grew by 250 per cent in the 1980s, and all areas of marketing services are currently experiencing growth. Television advertising has increased at the cost of radio and cinema. France has a successful pay TV channel – Canal Plus – with over two million subscribers. The press, however, remains the main medium with over 55 per cent of the total budget.

The classification of consumers is based on occupation.

Table 10.1   Population by social grade

	%
Management, executive	8.3
Senior management	5.7
White collar	11.1
Professional	13.5
Blue collar	21.6
Farmer	3.3
Retired	36.5

Source SECODIP, Chambourcy

The split in advertising in the media is approximately as follows:

Table 10.2   Media spend in France

	%
Newspapers	24
Magazines	26
TV	21
Radio	10
Outdoor	17
Cinema	2

Source IREP, Paris

Media

All media are subject to VAT at 18.6 per cent. Pharmaceutical advertisements must be approved by the health authorities and are subject to a tax of FF 1,000 when placed by the authority for examination. Tobacco advertisements are allowed in the press only, but the annual total amount of money allowed to be spent by tobacco products in the press is restricted according to a special formula based on previous investments. Copy in a tobacco advertisement can only name the product and show its packaging, composition, trade-mark and name and address of the manufacturer and/or distributor. Outdoor posters related to smoking are prohibited. Also, companies will be required to devote at least half their advertising budget to low-tar products. Targeting of children is strictly forbidden. Advertisements for alcoholic beverages are restricted in all media and forbidden on TV except for drinks up to and including 1° strength alcohol. All alcoholic advertising in sports grounds and all places where educational events take place is forbidden. Even where advertising is allowed in the press, a warning has to be included urging moderation in drinking. Also forbidden on TV are advertisements for the press, cinema, shows and retailers. For more information on advertising contact: Association des Agences Conseils en Publicité (AACP), 40 Boulevard Malesherbes, 75008 Paris (Tel: (+33) 1 4742 1342).

The spend rankings by key categories are:

Table 10.3   Key spend categories in France

(1) Household appliances
(2) Food
(3) Retail trade
(4) Leisure, entertainment
(5) Toiletries, beauty products
(6) Beverages
(7) Clothing
(8) Culture, tourism

Source SECODIP, Chambourcy

CONSUMER PREFERENCES/DIFFERENCES

Household spend

Although not as houseproud as the Belgians, the French level of spending on household products is high when compared to other countries in the EU. Domestic and household appliances (electrical sector) show that sales are 2 per cent higher than the Belgian spend.

As far as environmental issues are concerned, the French, Germans, Dutch and Italians are most aware and show the greatest concern and this is reflected in their purchase preferences of products and foods.

The French bask in the knowledge that they are considered to be the most chic and elegant of nations. Mute, pastel shades are common choices of colour not only in soft furnishings but in the colour schemes of other products, from household appliances to clothes.

The breakdown of household spending on domestic goods and services is as follows.

Table 10.4   French household spend

Items	%
Furniture (including carpets and other floor coverings)	31
White goods	16
Furnishings	7
Table utensils	15
Domestic and other household services	31

Source Eurostate/Mintel

Financial awareness

Over the last few years the French have become more sophisticated in financial matters; fast disappearing is the image of suitcases of gold stashed under the bed. Another example of this increased financial sophistication is that the French now have the highest level of purchase of unit trusts in the EU. Overall on investment, however, they consider savings to be at the bottom of their preference list.

Next to the Germans the French have the highest percentage of personal bank accounts. Major international banks have a presence in most provincial cities as well as Paris. Moreover, the French have the highest percentage of penetration of credit cards.

Food spend

The French method of shopping has changed quite radically over the last decade, showing a 24 per cent increase in the use of hypermarkets and supermarkets.

The French cuisine is known and enjoyed worldwide and the French are duly proud of this. Surprisingly however, fresh fruit consumption is lower than that found in Germany and the UK. Meat consumption figures show that France heads the league consumer table in canned meat and canned fish consumption, the spend on the former, per capita, is valued at approximately US$ 26 million. The French are at the top of the spend list in the EU for meat consumption, having equal taste for pork, beef and veal but overall spend more on fish than meat. Purchase of canned fruit and vegetables is also very high.

Per capita, France has the highest consumption of butter in the EU, and as would be expected cheese consumption is high, in fact the second highest in the EU.

Not unexpectedly as it is one of the major wine producers, France has a very strong home market and her wine consumption ranks among the highest in the EU.

General consumer spend

When given the opportunity to increase their spending, the first preference for the French is a day out or a holiday while the lowest desire is to save and investment. Credit is therefore an important and attractive consideration for the French when selecting which item/items to buy.

Belgium is the market leader in total purchasing volume of clothing, but the French are not far behind.

In the percentage spend on passenger cars, France is fourth behind Germany, Italy and England.

Political trends

The notable gains in the Euro election in France were made by the Green Party, who hold nine out of a total of 81 Euro seats. The 'green' issue is seen to be important.

France recorded 49 per cent voter turnout but is still below the average EU total of 59 per cent.

ESTABLISHING A BUSINESS

A foreign-owned enterprise in France has the same legal status as a French-owned one, and the government does not insist on French participation.

The two most important forms of company are the *Société Anonyme* (SA) and the Société à Responsabilité Limitée (SARL). The main difference between the two is that equity in the SARL is closely held, while in the SA it is not normally restricted to the founders of the company.

Every new enterprise must be registered in the Companies

and Commercial Register, giving information on its constitution and details concerning its offices. The lease on offices and sometimes the residence permit of the application.

New businesses must also report to the local direct and value added tax authorities and the social security office. A signed copy of the constitutional documents must be submitted to the registration duty authorities for payment of the duty.

A zone certificate, showing the company's proposed activity is permitted, must be obtained from the Ministry of the Environment in the department concerned. New buildings require a building permit from the mayor of the commune, plus, in Paris, the Ministry of the Environment. Local building controls are complex, and numerous anti-pollution measures are in force.

Management structure

A corporation may choose between two different systems of management:

1. a single administrative board (*conseil d'administration*) by a president who usually acts both as chairman of the board and chief executive of the corporation; or
2. a two-tier system comprising an executive committee (*directorie*) and an independent supervisory board (*conseil de surveillance*) which oversees the activities of the executive committee.

Very broadly, the functions of the chief executive in the single-tier system correspond with those of the executive committee in the two-tier system, and those of the administrative board in the two-tier system. A corporation may change from one form of management to the other by decision of the shareholders. The single-tier system is still the more widely used.

In the single-tier system, the administration board consists of three to twelve directors (*administrateurs*) who are elected by the shareholders. Larger boards are permitted in limited circumstances. The first directors of a private corporation may be named in the articles, in which case each serves for a maximum of three years. In all other cases, a director is elected for a maximum of six years.

Board members, including the president, are personally liable for any mismanagement of the corporation. Contracts between board members and their corporations must be specifically approved.

The supervisory board in the alternative two-tier system

consists of three to twelve members whose appointments and procedures are broadly similar to those of administrative board members under the single-tier system.

The executive committee consist of two to five members who are appointed by the supervisory board for fixed terms of four years. They may be removed from office only by the shareholders in general meeting on the advice of the supervisory board. Members of the committee do not have to be French nationals or shareholders, but must be individuals. The committee is responsible for the day-to-day management of the corporation and is given the widest powers of representation. It must submit a quarterly report on the corporation's activities to the supervisory board, and is responsible for producing year-end financial statements.

In the two-tier structure, only the president of the executive committee, if from a non-EU member state, needs to hold a commercial card.

Employees of at least two years' standing may be appointed as members of an administrative board, although not more than one-third of the members at any one time could have employment contracts with the corporation. The two years' standing requirement does not apply if the corporation is formed after 1 January 1988. Employees may not be members of a supervisory board but may be appointed to an executive committee.

Any corporation with 50 or more employees must establish a works committee (*comité d'entreprise*). This body may send two representatives to attend meetings of the administrative or supervisory boards, but not to meetings of the executive committee. These representatives have no voting rights at such meetings.

USEFUL ADDRESSES

Sources of information and help

French Chamber of Commerce
2nd Floor
Knightsbridge House
197 Knightsbridge
London SW7 1RB
Tel: 071-225 5254
Fax: 071-225 5557

British Consulates General in France
11 Square Duttileul
59800 Lille
Tel: (+33) 20 578790
Tel: 120169

Research sources

AC Nielsen
44 Boulevard de Grenelle
75737 Paris
Tel: (+33) 1 4578 5120
Tlx: 270868

Addresses for advertisers

Association des Agences Conseils en Publicité (French Association of Advertising Agencies)
40 Boulevard Malesherbes
75008 Paris
Tel: (+33) 1 4742 1342

Association Nationale du Marketing-Recherche et Strategie-Action (major marketing association)
Josette Lefeune
221 rue la Fayette
75010 Paris

Chambers of Commerce

Bordeaux	12 Place de la Bourse 33076 Bordeaux Tel: (+33) 56 909128
Lyon	Palais du Commerce Lyon Tel: (+33) 7 842 2575
Marseilles	Palais de la Bourse 13222 Marseilles Cedex 1 Tel: (+33) 91 919151
Nice	20 Boulevard Carabacal 06007 Nice Tel: (+33) 93 559155

Paris	Chambre de Commerce de Paris 27 Avenue de Friedland Paris Tel: (+33) 1 236 2438
Strasbourg	Place Gutenburg 67081 Strasbourg Tel: (+33) 88 321255
Toulouse	Palais Consulaire 2 rue d'Alsace-Lorraine BP 1506 31002 Toulouse Tel: (+33) 61 537200

Principle Euro Info Centres

Euroguichet
rue de la Republique 16
F-69289 Lyon Cedex 02
Tel: (+33) 78 38 1010

Euroguichet
Place St. Clement 1
BP 1004
F-57036 Metz Cedex 1
Tel: (+33) 87 33 60 00

Euroguichet
10 Place Gutenberg
F-67081 Strasbourg Cedex
Tel: (+33) 88 32 12 55

Euroguichet
Place de la Bourse 2
F-33076 Bordeaux Cedex
Tel: (+33) 56 52 65 47

Euroguichet
Centre des Salonges BP 718
16 Quai Ernest Renaud
F-44027 Nantes Cedex 04
Tel: (+33) 40 44 60 60

11
GERMANY

INTRODUCTION

The stereotyping of Germany as efficient, conscientious and formal is to a large extent relative. Although, after reunification, Berlin struggles to contain its costs, its premier position within Europe is under threat. Inflation is no longer lower than the UK's, unemployment is over 3 million and there is a growing budget deficit and surge in the money supply. After years of unparalleled prosperity the stark reality of unification and recession has yet to be accepted by the workforce, who, at the end of April 1992, staged their first major public sector strike for 18 years. In reality, Germany is not a cold nation controlled by the formality of its culture. Germans respond positively and creatively within a framework well known and understood. The crux of successful business relationships is reading the hidden agenda while responding to the surface normality.

The more Calvinistic North (Hamburg, Bremen and Hanover) tends to reflect the ethos of hard work and there is a serious attitude to life. Many people, particularly the elderly, maintain that the country has strayed into a more relaxed, lazier state, and there is some truth in this. Germany's workforce do put in fewer working hours than they once did: 20 per cent less in just over 15 years. On average, their working week is 20 per cent shorter than the Japanese, and they have longer holidays than the British. However, although there may have been a quantitative decrease, there is no sign of a qualitative deficiency. Work is tightly focused, with little time spent socialising and time-filling. This quality expectation is obvious in all aspects of business life, from the initial interview where small talk is seen as just that, to expectations of behaviour in business partners.

Germans are, however, surprisingly accommodating to the

'frailty' of other nations, provided, that is, they make adequate efforts. Germans, who have one of the highest levels of dual-language competency at board level in Europe, are able and willing to discuss business in a foreign language if they are proficient in it. However, in any such conversation you should always acknowledge the effort that the German is making and you should respond appropriately, by talking more slowly than usual, using fewer idioms and at all times being patient and polite.

To achieve business success in the German market you need to be very good at what you do, and maintain your achievement. If, for instance, your advantage is based upon technical superiority then should that be lost, so will the business.

Germans are accomplished and demanding commercial negotiators. They will require excellent business references, demonstrations of products, and evidence of some well-researched information as to their business needs.

The German's national prejudice towards other nations will also figure in the type of terms required in any deal. For British firms, tight delivery dates, high penalties for failure and generous warranty periods will usually be included in any contract. However, given satisfactory performance, a German client will pay on time and keep to the letter and spirit of any agreement.

MAKING THE APPOINTMENT

Formality is the key to a successful business relationship. It begins with establishing a rapport with the executive's secretary. (German secretaries really do see themselves as an extension of their bosses, and expect formality in all matters.) The initial contact is best received in a well written, personally-addressed letter. Because of the hierarchical nature of the German business culture, a letter addressed to a level senior to the one with whom you are likely to transact the contract will, if passed down, enhance the receptivity of the German negotiator.

The letter should be written in good business German. A poorly constructed letter will work against you. You should, when writing, use the impersonal address *Herr* or for women, married or single, *Frau*. Responses to letters should take about two weeks, after which a telephone enquiry is acceptable. If you are unable to speak German, the letter seeking a personal interview (Germans will expect to meet personally to conclude any serious business transactions) should state this, and you should offer to bring an interpreter to the meeting. If your

German host wishes to use his language, or if such an interpreting facility is available within the company, he will let you know.

Formality in the conduct of the meeting is as important as it is in the letter. You should avoid being late or, come to that, early. A German's diary is full, and an early arrival can be as disruptive as a late one. Expect everything to be arranged. Everyone, from the receptionist upwards, will know you are coming. Your visits will be arranged with great efficiency, but the pace may seem extremely slow.

THE MEETING

Be well prepared for the first, usually quite short, meeting. Your German counterpart will act as 'host'. Business-orientated opening comments (for example, 'you have a fine factory') are expected as small talk, not personal enquiries. It is polite and sensible to follow the lead of your host, responding to his speed, level of detail, and direction. To be seen to be uncomfortable or irritated at the rate of progress or level of detail would offend one of the unwritten rules. If you are using your own language, make sure you choose your words carefully, using simple linguistic constructions so as to flatter your host's skill in front of his junior colleagues.

It is possible that lunch will be offered, but notification of this will probably have been given before the meeting. If you have issued the invitation, you will be expected to pay.

One of the most striking elements of a German business meeting is the hand shaking which takes place. This occurs on every possible occasion, at the beginning and close of meetings and extends to everyone joining the meeting, and leaving midway through (although unexpected interruptions are unlikely to occur).

ENTERTAINING

Business meals

In Germany, business meals will almost exclusively be lunch or dinner, although German business people will start before the core business time of 9.00 am to 5.00 pm, or match industrial times. German style is to start work early, and meetings at 8.30 am are common, although banks (a major influence on business) are likely to keep meetings until after 9 o'clock in the morning. Lunch is likely to be taken early: 12.00–12.30 pm, and hardly ever will the meal commence after 1.00 pm. Alcohol is acceptable, but the extended business lunch has lost favour now. A simple pre-lunch drink and wine is the general rule.

Most middle to senior managers will be willing to accept lunch, although members of the *Vorstrand* (management board) may decline. Lunch is unlikely to take more than 90 minutes and more usually will last just one hour. Dinner or pre-dinner drinks at a German's home are an important sign of progression both in terms of business and personal relationships. In most cases, restaurant dinners are normal for quite a while in the relationship.

If visiting a German's house either for drinks or dinner, it is important to take flowers for the lady of the house. This custom is well known to German florists, who will construct an appropriate arrangement. A gift of wine, in addition, is becoming more common if you are dining at your German host's home, particularly if this is seen as part of your own tradition.

Although it is right and proper to shake the hand of your host, your hostess's hand should only be taken if extended. In German company, those well known to the hostess might kiss her extended hand; however, you should not do this until you know her well. It is expected that a few days after dinner you will send a brief 'Thank you' note.

Toasts at formal dinners are very short. The host will say just a few words of welcome, to which all those dining will respond by thanking him. If required, your response should be short and simple.

The Germans have a very close-knit business and social community. To break in to this takes time and patience; never to do so is common. An understanding of German culture, art and literature helps. The major corporations are still run by some of Germany's oldest money and by the banks. Deutsche Bank, for instance, is the largest bank and the largest shareholder in the largest company, Daimler-Benz. Banks and their attitude to investment – solid, low-risk attitudes – shape the philosophy of most companies.

Subjects for social discussion

Germans are well read and have a good understanding of world affairs. Education, environmental and individual development are issues for discussion. In many cases, the understanding that you should 'never mention the war' is likely to be pre-empted by it cropping up in your German host's conversation!

Business hospitality

Business hospitality is nowhere near as extravagant as in, say, the UK or France. Formal hospitality events are rare, and the Germans are unlikely to organise them outside working hours.

Gifts

These are welcome, provided they are seen as just that. A logoed pen, business folder or diary are acceptable, but expensive gifts cause embarrassment and are unwelcome.

Dress

Formality in dress, accompanied by overt cleanliness, is important on all occasions. Men wear plain suits, not necessarily dark, and white or blue shirts either plain or with a discreet stripe. Coloured shirts with white collars are accepted as 'British' but flamboyant ties and boldly striped shirts are viewed with suspicion. Clean shoes are also important, regardless of the weather conditions.

WOMEN IN BUSINESS

Only about 2 per cent of the major companies have women at senior levels. Those women who hold senior positions have usually inherited them from husbands or fathers, or have started the business themselves. This chauvinistic attitude to women is projected on to foreigners. Although a German businessman will be polite, he is likely to believe that the businesswoman is acting on behalf of a male colleague who will be consulted prior to any agreement being reached.

WORKING HOURS AND PUBLIC HOLIDAYS

The core business hours are 9.00 am–5.00 pm, although many executives will start as early as 8.00 am and finish after 6.00 pm. Germans have, on average, five weeks' holiday, of which three to four are likely to be taken in summer, during July and August.

Public holidays are:

1st January	(New Year's Day)
6th January	(Epiphany)
1st May	(Labour Day)
17th June	(National Unity Day)
15th August	(Assumption)
1st November	(All Saint's Day)
25th/26th December	(Christmas Day)

There are, in addition, six movable days, including Easter.

LETTER-WRITING

The envelope

German	English
Herr (initials[a], surname)	Mr
Frau (initials[a], surname)	Mrs
Fraulein (initials[a], surname)	Miss

Salutation

German	If the letter is written in: English
Sehr geehrter Herr (surname)	Dear Mr (surname)
Sehr geehrte Frau (surname)	Dear Mrs (surname)
Sehr geehrtes Fräulein (surname)	Dear Miss (surname)
Not used	Dear Sir
Sehr geehrte Damen und Herren	Dear Sirs

Closing
Individual: Mit freundlichen Grüssen	Yours sincerely
Company: Hochachtungsvoll	Your faithfully

Note
[a] The first forename may be used instead of an initial.

MARKETING

Germany's development as a marketing economic force is based upon four major facts:

1. social market economy;
2. membership of the EU;
3. anatomy of the *Bundesbank* and free money and capital movements;
4. accord between the trade unions and employers.

(This almost creates a national corporation: Government, unions and employers.)

These factors have led to an economy with a steady inflation rate, level unemployment and a controllable growth in GNP. In this environment advertising and media opportunities have grown. It is estimated by *Gasaintverbank Werkeagenturers* (GWA), the joint Advertising Agency Associations, that by the year 2000 the gross income of advertising agencies will triple from the 1985 figure, to DM 49.9 billion, which is just under DM 1,000 for each of the population.

Unlike the UK, there are no fixed socio-economic groups for marketing purposes. Target groups are defined in terms of sex, age, education, region, size of household and children in household. However, for purposes of defining an upper class (AB), German marketers usually use the following classification: household net minimum income of DM 3,000 a month, and head of household's educational level of at least High School graduation.

The split of advertising spend in the media is approximately as follows:

Table 11.1   Media spend in Germany

	%
Newspapers	28
Consumer magazines	38
Trade magazines	5
Television	16
Radio	7
Outdoor	5
(Media)	1

Source Nielsen

The spending rankings by key categories are:

Table 11.2   Key categories spend in Germany

(1) Travel, tourism
(2) Cosmetics, pharmaceuticals
(3) Food
(4) Beverages (alcoholic and non-alcoholic)
(5) Banks, insurance
(6) Household cleaners
(7) Clothing, textiles
(8) Tobacco
(9) Furniture

Source Nielsen

Media

There are no specific advertising taxes: VAT is charged at 14 per cent. Prescription drugs are not allowed to be advertised on any medium. Tobacco advertisements are not permitted on TV or radio. There are restrictions on the advertising of alcoholic beverages and on advertising aimed at children, or advertising which uses children. For further information, contact: Deutscher Werberat, ZAW, Postfach 200647, 5300 Bonn (Tel: 228 351025).

CONSUMER PREFERENCES/DIFFERENCES

Household spend

Germany is the EU's biggest consumer spender. The Germans 'spend total' on their purchase of goods (homes, clothes, etc) is more than any other EU nation. On home appliances, the Germans have the highest penetration of electrical goods except for stereos, where they are second to the UK, and leisure electrical goods. For example, there are more dishwashers, electric stoves and central heating systems sold in Germany than elsewhere in the Community.

The breakdown of the spend on household goods and services is as follows.

Table 11.3   Household spend in Germany

Items	%
Furniture (including carpets and other floor coverings)	29
White goods	25
Furnishings	9
Table utensils	13
Domestic and other household services	24

Source Eurostat/Mintel

Financial awareness

In common with most of Northern Europe, the Germans have a high penetration of bank usage. However, they prefer to pay cash for their purchases and so the level of penetration of credit cards is low. Being a consumer-hungry society, the volume of cash transaction is considerable, and supports a high technology trend in store equipment.

Over the last few years the Germans have taken the financial lead in Europe which could culminate in the European Central Bank being situated in their country.

The Germans are not as well served with other financial products as the British but are well ahead of their neighbours in the Netherlands.

Food spend

The Germans top the league table in the consumption of beverages drinking more beer, orange juice and coffee, and are second only to the Belgians in their consumption of mineral water. They drink more spirits than elsewhere in the Community.

The preference for meat products is high, roughly equal amounts of fresh and tinned are sold. Pork is their favourite meat and there are many varied products.

General consumer spend

More cars are bought in Germany than elsewhere and the same is true of bicycles.

The Germans are environmentally-aware, with consumer selections of 'green' products taking priority over others. The Germans tend to be more health conscious but this is seen not necessarily in the reduction of their fat and drink intake but more in the preference for physical exercise.

Political trends

The excitement and optimism of unification in 1990 seems now to be a bitter economic pill for the government to swallow. The government has not done well in recent local elections where a growth in support for right wing pressure groups has been evident.

Voter participation in Germany is above the EU average showing a turnout of 62 per cent.

ESTABLISHING A BUSINESS

Every new enterprise must report its intention to commence business to the local economic supervisory office (*Wirtschafts und Ordnungsamt*) in the municipality concerned, which will issue a certificate of registration (*Gewerbeanmeldeschein*). Some industries (for example, food, pharmaceutical and medical products, banks, insurance companies and transport) require special licences. Proof of the qualifications or reliability of those concerned must be produced; without such proof, an examination conducted by a Chamber of Commerce or other body must be passed.

Every new business must register with the Commercial Register (*Handelsregister*) maintained at the local court, the municipal trade tax office (Stadtsteueramt), the local tax office (*Finanzamt*), and (as soon as employees are engaged) the local social security office (*Allgemeine Ortskrankenkasse*). It must also join the Chamber of Commerce in the area in which its head office is situated. Any enterprise in which a non-resident makes an investment, whether by partial or complete acquisition or (in many cases) by way of a loan, must report the investment to the Federal Reserve Bank through the appropriate state central bank, unless it is only DM 20,000 or less in any year.

Building permits are required for the construction of new buildings. In some industries a special licence may be required to construct or occupy particular types of industrial buildings.

There are two types of limited liability company; the private *Gesellschaft mit beschränkter Haftung* (GmbH), and the public limited, *Aktiengesellschaft* (AG). AGs are set up by large, corporate enterprises who wish for large scale public participation. Small to middle-sized businesses would find it difficult to make the administrative and financial outlays to comply with the Company's Act. The minimum capitalisation of a GmbH is DM 50,000, whereas an AG requires DM 100,000. Although both types of company issue share certificates, this is not a requirement for a GmbH.

Management structure

The business of a limited liability company is conducted by one or more managing directors (*Geschäftsführer*), who need not be German nationals or residents, nor need they be members. In an AG, this is done by the Board of Directors (*Vorstand*). Among other duties, the managers are responsible for maintaining the company's statutory records and for the preparation of financial statements. An individual manager's power to bind the company in transactions with third parties, however, cannot be effectively limited, except by requiring joint signatures — either of two managers or of one manager and a managing employee (*Prokurist*). Managers are personally liable to the company and its members for any damage caused by unauthorised acts. They are also liable to fines or imprisonment if they fail to declare a bankruptcy within three weeks of learning that the company is insolvent, and the company continues to incur liability. A non-resident manager should appoint a resident deputy who will be answerable to the authorities for the proper conduct of the company.

A public or private limited liability company is required to have a supervisory board (*Aufsichtsrat*), in addition to a board of managers, if the number of its employees regularly exceeds 500. A smaller company may provide for a supervisory board in its articles of association, if it so wishes. If the supervisory board is a mandatory one, one-third of the members must be elected by the employees, the other two-thirds being elected by the shareholders. If there are more than 2,000 employees, one-half of the members must be elected by the employees and the supervisory board must appoint a labour director or personnel manager (*Arbeitsdirektor*) to the board of managers. In situations where a compromise seems unlikely, the chairman, elected either by a two-thirds vote of the board or by the shareholders' board members alone, has a casting vote. The function of a supervisory board is to oversee the company's activities. It may also be required to give prior approval to major decisions taken by the managers. Members of the board need not be German nationals or residents.

Employees of a company with more than five employees have the right to establish a works council (*Betriebsrat*). This consists of elected representatives of all the employees. The functions of a works council include the consideration of social, personnel and economic policies. Its approval is required for decisions affecting employment, such as mergers, plant relocations or changes in production methods. A company with over 100 employees must also set up an 'economic committee' (*Wirtschaftsausschuss*). Such a committee comprises a small number of management and employee representatives with the right to receive and discuss periodic information on sales, production and financial matters. The committee is consultative only and does not have the power to approve or disapprove of activities.

USEFUL ADDRESSES

Sources of information and help

*Austellungs – und Messe – Ausschuss der
   Deutschen Wirtschaft AG* (Confederation
   of German Trade Fair and Exhibition
   Industries)
Lindenstrasse 8,
D-5000 Koln 1
Tel: (+49) 221 209070

British Chamber of Commerce in Germany
The Secretariat
Heumarkt 14
D-5000 Cologne 1
Tel: (+49) 221 234284
Tlx: 8883400 FIBLD

*British Marketing Office (Advanced
   Technology)*
Kronprinzstrasse 14
7000 Stuttgart 1
Tel: (+49) 711 294562
Tlx: 722 397
Fax: 0711 229271

Bundesverband den Deutschen Industrie (BDI),
   (Federation of German Industry)
Gustav-Heinemann-Upr 84–88
Postfach 510548
D-5000 Koln 51
Tel: (+49) 221 370800

Deutscher Industrie - und Handelsrat (DHIT)
   (Federation of German Chambers of Commerce)
Abernaveneralle 148
D-5300 Bonn 1

German Chamber of Industry and Commerce
16 Buckingham Gate
London SW1E 6LB
Tel: 071-233 5656
Fax: 071-233 7835

Research sources

A C Nielsen Company
PO Box 160531
Ludwig Laudmann Strasse 405
D-6000 Frankfurt am Main 16
West Germany
Tel: (+49) 69 79380
Tlx: 412031

ADM-Arbeitskreis Deutscher
   Marktforschungsin (Market Research
   Assocation)
Papenkamp 2–6
2410 Molln
Tel: (+49) 4542 801 216

Addresses for advertisers

Gesellschaft Werbeagenturen (German advertising
   agencies body)
Friedenstrasse 11
D-6000 Frankfurt am Main
Tel: (+49) 69 235096

Interessengemeinschaft Deutscher Fachmessen
   und Austellungsstadte (Trade Fair organisers)
Margaretenstrasse 4
D 7000 Stuttgart 60
Tel: (+49) 711 335629

Chambers of Commerce

Berlin	Hardenbergstrasse 16–18 Berlin 12 Tel: (+49) 30 31801
Bonn	Bonner Talweg 17 Bonn Tel: (+49) 228 22840
Bremen	Am Markt 13 Bremen Tel: (+49) 421 36371
Cologne	Unter Sachsenhausen 10–26 Cologne 1 Tel: (+49) 221 16401

Dortmund	Märkische Strasse 120 Dortmund Tel: (+49) 231 54170
Dusseldorf	Ernst-Schneider-Platz 1 Dusseldorf Tel: (+49) 211 35371
Frankfurt	Börensplatz Frankfurt Tel: (+49) 69 21971
Hamburg	Adlophsplatz 1 Hamburg 11 Tel: (+49) 40 361380
Hanover	Berliner Allee 25 Hanover Tel: (+49) 511 31071)
Munich	Max-Josephastrasse 2 Munich Tel: (+49) 89 51161
Nuremberg	Hauptmarkt 25 Nuremberg Tel: (+49) 911 13350
Stuttgart	Jägerstrasse 30 Stuttgart Tel: (+49) 711 20051

Principle Euro Info Centres

EG-Beratungsstelle für Unternehmen
Dohne 54
D-4330 Mulheim Ruhr
Tel: (+49) 208 300 04 31

EG-Beratungsstelle für Unternehmen
Helwigstrasse 33
D-2000 Hamburg 20
Tel: (+49) 40 460 20 87

EG-Beratungsstelle für Unternehmen
Adenauer Allee 148
Postfach 1446
D-5300 Bonn 1
Tel: (+49) 228 10 40

EG-Beratungsstelle für Unternehmen
D. Martin Luther Strasse 12
Postfach 110 355
D-8400 Regensburg
Tel: (+49) 941 569 41

12
GREECE

INTRODUCTION

The Greeks are justifiably proud of their history and role as the first centre of European civilisation. This pride is reflected in their manner of doing business; they are always trustworthy, although they can be erratic. The Greek is also sometimes covert, or even insecure, which is shown in his tendency to play his cards close to his chest, keep a few tricks up his sleeve, play-act, bargain, call bluffs and generally make a business associate feel like a co-conspirator. Suspicion of the state is another trait; to the Greeks, the state is not a partner in national development, but a foe to outwit at every turn.

The Greek mentality has little preference for long-term industrial projects and is more suited to trade. Most manufacturing companies are family-owned and, although likely to have well-trained businesspeople on the staff, they will still react best to business propositions put to them by people who have spent time establishing a relationship with them.

The Greek temperament is complex; the Athenian character is described by Thucydides as 'one man's success is tolerable only when others feel they could have done it themselves'. Never exert too much pressure on the Greeks; they will react at their own pace and as they see fit. The Greeks object to gross exhibition of money or personal discussion of the subject.

Greece can be many things to businesspeople, the Greece, that is, of Athens and Piraeus, at any rate. It can mean engaging agents to secure, for example, official approval from the relevant government ministers, and provide important liaison and formal introduction to Greek counterparts. And it can mean wonderful people and warm, lovely weather. But remember, Greece is a hard place to do business, built on a notion of who you know, and on handouts.

MAKING THE APPOINTMENT

An introduction from an acceptable institution, company or associate is the key to doing business in Greece. Where this is not immediately available, organisations such as the British Hellenic Chamber of Commerce in Athens can facilitate the introduction. This introduction can be personal or in the form of a letter to be presented at the first meeting.

Having secured an introduction, your Greek counterpart can be approached by telephone or letter to secure an appointment. The letter could be in Greek, but the Greek businessperson is aware of the complexity of the language and will be prepared to accept a letter written in the mother language of the businessperson. If you choose the letter route, however, beware. Greeks dislike letter-writing and may well ignore the nicety of a written response. Telephone after a couple of weeks to ensure your request has been received. You may offer an interpreter, but this may not be necessary, as Greeks generally speak good English, French and German. Greek translation is very difficult.

The role of the secretary varies in large and small companies. In large multinationals, a modern, complementary role is exercised. In small companies the boss will arrange everything in his own way. Everything that has to be done is done through him. However, the route for communication can be directly to the functional head, if he exists. It is very unlikely that an executive will react without senior discussion and reference.

THE MEETING

Once a meeting has been set up, it is best to keep the discussion formal in nature. The Greeks shake hands as frequently as most Europeans and will treat you with great courtesy, offering refreshment. Be fully prepared for the meeting and know your – and their – business well.

The Greeks, if they have time, like to get to know the person with whom they are doing business, and they may spend some time in small talk, effectively summing you up. Do not try to bring the subject back to business, as this will only antagonise them. At all times follow their lead, but do not be afraid to haggle; not only will the Greek businessperson feel cheated intellectually if you accept his intial offer, he will also distrust you.

Contracts are best left to lawyers and will be explicit. The Greeks having once made the deal, will honour it, except when (and this is a dying habit) he thinks he can improve upon it for you. This improvement in specification might well be made unilaterally, so it is wise to keep an eye on production. The

Greeks will sue very quickly if your end of the contract is unfulfilled. The speed of their actions is not only driven by their own desire to be paid, but also by the Central Bank who, having given special approval for foreign currency deals (Greece still has exchange controls), want to see evidence of the business transaction as soon as possible.

Gaining an interview indicates a potential need to do a deal. It is not unknown for Greek companies to receive orders or enquiries for products which, because they are at current full capacity, will be ignored. Such is the immediacy of the Greeks that they will not even offer a letter of explanation or attempt to preserve the order for another year.

If business is successfully completed, take care in congratulating your Greek colleagues on the detail of your agreement: the Greeks will never be really sure they have struck a good deal, and reference to it will tend to raise suspicion rather than establish mutual harmony.

The Greeks are a friendly people, and even have an ancient god of hospitality to foreigners; however, do not try to break with formality too quickly.

ENTERTAINING

Business meals

Greeks eat little during the morning and early evening. The breakfast meeting does not exist in Greece, because the Greeks do not take breakfast! And they begin work at 7.00 am in the summer. Lunch is also taken late, in Athens around 3.00–3.30 pm – the end of the working day. Greeks in the provinces will go home for lunch, which will be light, and then take a siesta for two hours. In the cities, lunch may be taken in a restaurant; if this is suggested it is a sign of growing warmth in the relationship.

The main business entertainment meal is dinner. This will be taken any time from 9.00 to 9.30 pm and for those active enough can last until 2.00 am! Business may well be concluded over dinner and, if so, accept it. Congratulate your partner on a good deal and take whatever is offered in the way of hospitality.

Dining out is the preferred way of entertaining, but if you are invited home this is still further recognition of your importance. A request to join the family at the weekend must be accepted. If attending the home, flowers are appropriate or chocolates (a sign of Europeanism – both major Greek chocolate manufacturers have been recently bought out by Nestlé and Suchard).

The Greeks are far from the most punctual of people, but be on time yourself as a matter of courtesy.

Subjects for social discussion

Greeks are expansive and individual. Corporate entertainment takes on a very personal character. Small groups of business-people might be invited to a yacht for the evening, or a weekend cruise. This, however, is difficult to distinguish from personal entertainment, and should be treated with the same respect.

Gifts

The practice of giving gifts to secure a good relationship is now almost obsolete. A good quality item which is not ostentatious would be accepted if a particularly high level of service or assistance had been given. This should not, of course, (nor should it seem to) be linked to the outcome of a particular business transaction.

Dress

Formal dress is not always important in Greece. Men will wear open-necked shirts and trousers, women dresses and skirts (women do not normally wear trousers). In senior business meetings and for most directors, lightweight business suits will be worn. Unlike many countries, the cut of your counterpart's suits will not necessarily identify his status, so do not judge him by his clothes.

WOMEN IN BUSINESS

Women are seen as a very powerful influence behind the scenes and at home. Women who graduate are usually directed towards medicine and the caring professions. In Greece today, the main role of women is still considered to be as wives and mothers, and career women are treated with suspicion.

WORKING HOURS AND PUBLIC HOLIDAYS

Athens works summer and winter times. In the summer, work begins at 7.00 am and finishes at 3.00 pm; winter hours are 7.30 am to 3.30 pm. Remember, there is no real lunch break, except for a snack break at about 10.30 am. These times change in Piraeus. Being a major international port, it is supported by staff to match Northern European, American and Japanese time zones.

Businesspeople are prepared to take business calls at home, but usually only after 5.30–6.00 pm.

Public holidays are

1st January	(New Year's Day)
6th January	(Epiphany)
25th March	(Independence Day)
1st May	(Labour Day)
15th August	(Assumption Day)
26th October	(St Dimitrius's Day (Salonica))
28th October	(Ochi (No) Day)
25th December	(Christmas Day)
26th December	(St Stephen's Day)

There are in addition three movable days, including Good Friday and Easter Monday.

LETTER-WRITING

The Greeks accept the uniqueness of their language, and are not resentful of those people who are unable to write or speak it. Letters are best written in English, as most Greeks accept this as the main business language. British letter-writing conventions should be followed. However, French and German are both popular business languages, and if previous contact has established either of these as a common tongue, use the appropriate letter-writing conventions for the language chosen. Forenames or initials may be used on the envelope, and the business card is, as always, a good indicator of how the recipient likes to be addressed.

MARKETING

The advertising industry in Greece is emerging from its infancy into adolescence, mainly due to the Government's lifting of price controls in 1985. The result has seen heavy investment by marketing-oriented firms, both local and international. The move towards liberalisation within the framework of the EU is also reflected in the move towards the launching of private and municipal radio and TV stations. The development will significantly influence advertising strategies in created segment markets, with new media research and more educated and specialised marketing people.

The socio-economic profile of Greece may be broken down into three main sectors:

Table 12.1   Socio-economic profile in Greece

	%
Upper	14
Middle	39
Lower	41

Source Nielsen Hellas

The marketing spend is split as follows:

Table 12.2   Marketing spend in Greece

	%
Newspapers	14
Magazines	24
Radio	6
TV	50
Posters	6

Source Nielsen Hellas

The spend rankings by key categories are:

Table 12.3   Spend rankings in Greece

(1) Food and drink
(2) Toiletries
(3) Retail
(4) Household products
(5) Automotive
(6) Clothing

Source Publicity Guide

Media

VAT at 6 per cent was introduced in January 1987. Consumer advertisements for pharmaceutical products and cigarettes are not allowed on TV or radio, nor are advertisements for toys. Cigarettes and toys are, however, allowed to be advertised in the press and outdoors. Agency commission for all media is 20 per cent. The Greek Advertising Agencies Association operates its own code of conduct for its members. For further information contact: Greek Advertising Agencies Association, 12 Ravine Street, Athens (Tel: (+30) 1 722 6990).

CONSUMER PREFERENCES/DIFFERENCES

Household spend
Purchase of household equipment in Greece is one of the lowest in EU except for stoves, fridges and deep freezes.

Greece is a relative newcomer to the EU and as such there are few comparative consumption figures available.

Financial awareness
Few Greeks have bank accounts and the penetration of credit cards is low.

Food spend
The Greeks have increased their meat consumption by nearly 10 per cent in the past 10 years. They have one of the highest levels of consumption of mutton, lamb and goat in the EU; fish is popular and is eaten as much as the total of beef, veal and pork combined.

More cheese is consumed in Greece than in any other member state although France is not far behind in percentage terms. Second only to Italy, the Greeks consume more bread and pasta products than fellow states.

Drink consumption is equally divided in volume between beer and wine.

General consumer spend
One of the lowest spend levels of penetration in Greece is on clothing.

Percentage of passenger cars sold in the second lowest in the EU.

Greece ranks after Portugal and Spain in the trend towards the introduction of international shops.

Political trends
Local issues rather than Community ones (a trend followed in a number of EU member states' voting patterns) led the Socialists (and the Communists) to lose one seat.

The voter turnout in Greece was 78 per cent.

ESTABLISHING A BUSINESS

The Greek government is currently removing the controls on imported capital for direct investment, in line with EU currency regulations. The establishment of a business presence in Greece requires no permission from the authorities unless the planned investment is in manufacturing or incentives, in which case approval of the Ministry of National Economy is required.

A foreign enterprise may be established in Greece either as a subsidiary or as a branch. If a subsidiary is used, it is more usually an *Anonymi Eteria* (AE) or private company rather than an *Eterio Periorismensis Efthinis* (EPE) or public company.

Approval for the establishment and registration of both subsidiaries and branches must be obtained from the competent prefecture of the district in which the business will be located. An AE needs two shareholders (who may be foreigners) and a minimum capital of five million drachmae. The annual financial statements must be filed and, in the case of a subsidiary, published.

If a branch is set up, the foreign company must have a capital of five million drachmae if it is a corporation, or 200,000 drachmae if it is a limited liability company.

Management structure

Ownership of the smaller EPE is in the hands of 'quota holders'. No share certificates are issued, only quota certificates. The Clerk of the Court holds the registration book of quota holders. The company is managed by one or more administrators, or the founders. The administrator(s) can be appointed through the articles of association, or by a general meeting of quota holders. Once appointed, he can bind the company in contracts and, if he is appointed in the memorandum, he can only be dismissed for serious reasons by a court decision.

The larger AEs tend to be state-controlled and are managed by a board of at least three directors. They meet at least once a month and decide on matters concerning the administration and the management of the company's assets. Directors have an obligation of confidentiality when information relating to the company is given to them.

USEFUL ADDRESSES

Sources of information and help

British Embassy
1 Ploutarchou Street
Athens GR-106 75
Tel: (+30) 1 7236211
Tlx: 216440
Fax: 301 724 1872

Department of Trade and Industry
Exports to Europe Branch
1 Victoria Street
London SW1H 0ET
Tel: 01-215 5103 (Greece desk, capital goods)
      01-215 4776 (Greece desk, consumer goods)

Research sources

A C Nielsen Hellas Ltd (annual media survey,
    ad hoc services)
2 Charokopou Street
GR-17671 Kallithea
Athens
Tel: (+30) 1 958 8771
Tlx: 219098

Addresses for advertisers

Greek Advertisers' Association
46 Venizelou Avenue
GR-17676 Kallithea
Athens
Tel: (+30) 1 958 4383

Greek Association of Advertising Agencies
12 Ravine Street
GR-11521 Athens
Tel: (+30) 1 772 6990

Chambers of Commerce

Athens   British-Hellenic Chambers of Commerce
                  25 Vas Sofias Avenue
                  GR-10674
                  Athens
                  Tel: (+30) 1 721 0361/721 0493

                  Greek Chamber of Commerce and Trade
                  Akadimiai
                  10671 Athens
                  Tel: (+30) 1360 2567

Salonica   Chamber of Commerce
                  Tsimiskis 27–29
                  Salonica

Principal Euro Info Centres

Euro Info Centre
Morihovon Square 1
GR-54625 Thessaloniki
Tel: (+30) 31 53 98 17

Euro Info Centre
Yenias Street 16
GR-11528 Athens
Tel: (+30) 1 770 06 54

Euro Info Centre
7 Academias
GR-10671 Athens
Tel: (+30) 1 362 7337

13
IRELAND

INTRODUCTION

Ireland advertises itself as the European capital for skilled, youthful people. Whether this is quite right is debatable, but what is true is that one of Ireland's major assets is its well-educated, mobile young workforce.

The Republic of Ireland is separate from Northern Ireland, which is part of the UK, and this fact must never be forgotten. (Discussion on the subject should only be between the Irish.) The Republic itself is split between the urban areas, where the pace of life is faster, and 'the country' where the idealistic, pastoral image of Irish rural life can be a reality. The Irish have a well-developed sense of humour which they are not afraid to turn back upon themselves; the butt of their jokes are their own Kerry men.

The business language is English, although many people have learned Gaelic at school and may use it in conversation with other Irish – do not be tempted to join in.

The Irish drive on the same side of the road as the British, the buildings have a similar appearance and the people speak English. They are, however, never to be considered English. They should be given the same attention and care as dealing with any other foreign European country. The culture is rich and already they are probably more European than the British. They fully understand the stereotype of them held by the British; slow, provincial and slightly dull: the Irish are amongst the brightest and sharpest dealers you are ever likely to meet. They are liable to take offence easily and, because of the concentration in major urban areas (particularly Dublin) you should be careful what you discuss and with whom. Dublin has been likened to the largest village in Europe and this seems to be very true, with friendship, family and education networks linking most senior executives in one way or another.

Finally, avoid the written or verbal use of the word Eire; although it is the Gaelic for Ireland, it is only acceptable if the sender of the letter has written it all in that language and speaks it. If written in English, a letter should be addressed to the Republic of Ireland.

MAKING THE APPOINTMENT

Initial contact by letter is expected, although the telephone call followed up by a letter is acceptable. In most major companies the secretary will hold the diary and can arrange appointments. She is one with whom to develop a rapport. In small companies, or when an introduction has been given by another Irish businessman, then a direct and informal telephone call to your counterpart is acceptable. Always confirm in writing. Letter-writing conventions are the same as in the UK.

THE MEETING

At the meeting, be prepared for a fairly informal discussion: those who enter directly into business negotiations are not looked upon favourably. The Irish will move very quickly to using first names, even at the initial meeting, and will enjoy elements of the discussion which are outside the business theme. This more social approach to business means that appointments can take much longer than planned, and your travel plans or subsequent appointments should be taken into account.

The Irish are less inclined to get into complex legal discussions, and wish to agree a deal in principle rather than be bothered, initially, with the detail. Be prepared for a change once formal proposals are submitted. They will question and seek clarification on all points, and even try to renegotiate partially at this stage, if it suits them, away from the original principles. Also, do not be fooled by their general openness and friendship. You should not drop your guard, although you should seem to take it all at face value.

You cannot be confident that a deal is secure until the documents are signed. Once this is done, the Irish are committed and will deliver. This is where the networking can work negatively: if a business transaction is poorly honoured many will know about it, which will have an adverse effect on the standing of the businessperson concerned.

It is easy to make contact with senior figures in the media for PR purposes. Do not do this without a strong public relations consultant. The Irish media are among the most professional and ruthless in the world.

ENTERTAINING

Business meals

Breakfast meetings are becoming more common, owing largely to the American influence.

Lunch will be a normal extension of any business which occurs at that time, and is taken during 12.30–1.30 pm. The tax system has removed tax relief on lavish business entertaining, so if you invite, expect to pay. It is unlikely that an expensive lunch will be arranged; in Dublin a gentleman's club, hotel or yacht club are acceptable venues. Drinking has been cut considerably at lunchtime: expect one drink and one bottle of wine. In total, the lunch should take no more than an hour and a half.

Dinner is a wholly different event. The Irish reputation for good conversation and hospitality is fuelled by the excellence of the stout (Guinness in Dublin and Murphy's in Limerick) and the gregarious nature of the Irish. Do not be surprised to find yourself sitting next to a government minister or at least a close friend of one. It pays to know who they are in advance. In a restaurant, the true feel of an Irish village emerges, with mealtime conversation interrupted by the Irish counterpart's acknowledgement of his friends and peers. Business is usually conducted before dinner or early on; the real purpose of the meal is to evaluate people upon whom the final decision will be made. For this reason you should keep your wits about you and not get too carried away with the entertainment.

In most countries, invitations to the home convey a sense of acceptance. Ireland is no exception and if invited to a business partner's home you should certainly accept. For the hostess, flowers or chocolates are favourites and the host, because of high taxation, will appreciate duty-free spirits or wine.

Subjects for social discussion

The family, car, house and culture are the foundations of conversation. Avoid politics and religion unless asked, and even then try to remain neutral. Sport has a strong following in Ireland and a knowledge of international Irish sports personalities will impress. It is not wise to criticise the Irish, even in jest, or if they themselves initiate it; to join in can sour a relationship. Self-criticism is acceptable.

Business hospitality

This is a growing phenomenon in the Republic. It is acceptable for large Irish and international companies to support the arts and sport. Because of the scarcity of tickets for good quality sporting events, they should be accepted if at all possible. The Irish attitude to entertainment should be remembered, and a local hotel room booked!

At cultural events, spouses will attend and you are likely to receive an invitation for your partner. It is essential though you should take someone along.

Gifts

Initially, these are closely restricted to business-endorsed objects. However, it is possible, as your relationship develops – particularly with middle or lower management – that a bottle of duty-free spirits would be welcomed.

Dress

Convention is the key. The Irish individuality as a nation does not go as far as breaking with British conventions of dress, and adhering to these conventions will ensure no embarrassments. Women and young people as a whole dress very well and stylishly. Flamboyance is avoided, as are the excesses of female dress, such as mini skirts.

WOMEN IN BUSINESS

Women's role in commerce and industry still suffers from the restrictive stereotyping, often prevalent in Catholic countries, of women as child-raisers. Promotions will thus generally go to men, who are likely to have a more 'stable' employment record.

WORKING HOURS AND PUBLIC HOLIDAYS

Working hours in general are the same as in the UK, 9.00 am–5.30 pm, Monday to Friday. However, there is a growing tendency for executives to start early and work late, though less so than in the UK. The Irish businessperson likes to separate business from family life, but is prepared to take work home and receive office calls at home. Usually holiday entitlement is four to five weeks, which will normally be taken as one main holiday in the summer.

The following are public holidays:

1st January	(New Year's Day)
17th March	(St Patrick's Day)
25th December	(Christmas Day)
26th December	(St Stephen's Day)

There are, in addition, five movable days, including Good Friday and Easter Monday.

LETTER-WRITING

Gaelic is a live language for most Irish people, although none will expect to conduct business in it. In almost every case, a letter following UK conventions will be appropriate.

MARKETING

The main media operative in Ireland include RTE (radio and television), both operating a two-channel service, and the national press which currently consists of four daily, three evening and four Sunday papers, backed by the provincial press. Growth areas are outdoor advertising and exhibitions. Direct response has lagged behind the rest of Europe, but changes in the An Post (Post Office) should encourage greater use. Radio is of particular significance in the Irish market, holding an estimated 12 per cent of advertising, due mainly to the fact that state radio has always carried commercials.

The socio-economic breakdown is similar to that of the UK and uses the same definitions, with the addition of two categories: F50 and F50 + which denote farmers who own more or less than 50 acres.

Table 13.1   Socio-economic breakdown in the Republic of Ireland

	%
AB	9
C1	20
C2	22
D	22
E	7
F50—	10
F50+	10

Source JNMR

The media pound is spent in the following way:

Table 13.2   Media spend in Ireland

	%
Newspapers	34
Magazines	9
TV	37
Radio	12
Outdoor	8

Source ASI

The spend rankings by key categories are:

Table 13.3   Key spend rankings in Ireland

(1) Food, dairy products and confectionery
(2) Financial
(3) Motor trade
(4) Alcoholic beverages
(5) Personal hygiene
(6) Agriculture
(7) Clothing

Source ASI

Media

All media advertising is subject to VAT at 25 per cent, but can be reclaimed as a legitimate expense by registered advertisers. Agency commission is 15 per cent for magazines, 12.5 per cent for most national newspapers and 15 per cent for broadcast media. Advertising of cigarettes and spirits is not permitted on TV, radio or in the cinema. A code of advertising standards for Ireland lists a range of products for which there are restrictions and special recommendations. There is also a special code for radio and TV. For more information, contact: Advertising Standards Authority for Ireland, IPC House, 35/39 Shelbourne Road, Dublin 4 (Tel: 010 353 1 608766); and for radio and TV: RTE, Donnybrooke, Dublin 4 (Tel: 010 353 1 693111).

CONSUMER PREFERENCES/DIFFERENCES

Household spend

Although the Irish, *per capita*, spend less on consumption of durables, food, etc, than most of the EU member states, there are a few areas where the spend percentage is high. One of those areas is on the household. More specifically, there is a growing trend in purchasing of electrical household goods.

Financial awareness

All the major international banks have a presence in Dublin, although penetration by credit cards is not high. One of the causes could be that there is a noticeable age gap (20 to 40 year olds) in Ireland's human resources.

The Irish Government tried to encourage international finance houses to open offices in Ireland in preparation for 1992. It will be interesting to see what market penetration, if any, this may have on the home community.

Food spend

Ireland's consumption records for food are in potatoes and beer. It is one of the few countries in the Community where a sizeable volume of tea is drunk.

Meat consumption in Ireland ranks sixth in the Community with a market share of 1.15 per cent. Roughly speaking, the Irish consume equal amounts of all the main meat products. Although they eat relatively low levels of cheese, the Irish are the second highest consumers of butter in the Community.

General consumer spend

The lowest number of cars is sold in Ireland. But the Japanese presence in car sales represents as much as 40 per cent.

Clothes also have a low spend priority in Ireland and again this can relate to the human resource problem.

Political trends

With Ireland holding her national elections on the same day as the Euro elections (as in Greece), voter reaction was bound to be somewhat clouded by local rather than EU issues. Both Fianna Fail and Fine Gael lost two seats each. Ireland has a total of 15 Euro seats.

ESTABLISHING A BUSINESS

It is not necessary to obtain approval from the Irish Government before setting up a business in Ireland, although exchange-control requirements must be satisfied.

A foreign company may operate in Ireland either by establishing an Irish subsidiary, usually a private company, or a branch.

Every Irish company, and an overseas company establishing a place of business in Ireland, must submit its memorandum of association (charter) and articles of association (by-laws), translated into English where necessary, together with certain other particulars to the Registrar of Companies. Irish limited liability companies must file audited financial statements each year. It is not permissable for a corporation to be a director of an Irish incorporated company.

Business may also be conducted in Ireland through a partnership. If this is the case, the income will be taxed in the hands of the individual partners. Although unusual, it is also possible for a trust to trade in Ireland. However, trading trusts are subject to income tax at the rate of 35 per cent and are also liable for a 20 per cent surcharge on undistributed income of the trust.

Most Irish companies are private companies, that is they have less than 50 members and there are certain restrictions as to the transfer of shares or debentures. There is no minimum amount of share capital, but there must be at least two shareholders. Where such companies wish to receive government grants, the government body will normally request that there is a certain level of shareholders' equity in the company. They generally insist that an amount of equity, in the form of either share capital or subordinated loan, equal to the amount of grants received, must be injected into the company.

Management structure

For private companies, the memorandum and articles of association give the company structure (no qualifications are needed). By law, all companies must have two directors and a secretary. The directors can have wide powers of decision-making, and many articles are written to restrict this power in favour of the shareholders. There is no legal requirement for board meetings, but any director can call a meeting which must be held, provided sufficient notice is given. Decisions at board level are taken by majority vote, with a quorum of directors being two.

Employee representation for public and private companies is a matter for local negotiation; there is no legal requirement. Worker participation does exist at board level in some state industries. As in private companies, the actual internal structure of the company's management is a matter for internal rules. The same basic legal requirements apply to private as well as to public companies.

USEFUL ADDRESSES

Sources of information and help

Irish Embassy
17 Grosvenor Place
London, SW1X 7HR
Tel: 071-235 2171

Research sources

Market Research Bureau of Ireland Ltd
    (consumer research, media research)
MRBI House
43 Northumberland Avenue
Dun Laoghaire
Co. Dublin
Tel: 010 353 1 804661

Addresses for advertisers

Advertising Standards Authority for Ireland
IPC House
35/39 Shelbourne Road
Dublin 4
Tel: 010 353 1 608766

Association of Advertisers in Ireland
44 Lower Leeson Street
Dublin 2
Tel: 010 353 1 761016

Institute of Advertising Practitioners in Ireland
35 Upper Fitzwilliam Street
Dublin 2
Tel: 010 353 1 765991
Tlx: 93381

Chamber of Commerce

Dublin   7 Clare Street
                         Dublin 2
                         Tel: 010 353 1 612888

Principal Euro Info Centres

European Business Information Centre
Merrion Hall
PO Box 203
Strand Road
Sandymount
Dublin 4
Tel: 010 353 1 695011

European Business Information Centre
The Granary
Michael Street
Limerick
Tel: 010 353 1 640777

14
ITALY

INTRODUCTION

After Greece, Italy could surely claim to be the epicentre of Western culture, with its great cities of Rome, Florence and Venice. However, until recently Italy tended to be a fragmented country, lacking in the national consciousness of most other major European nations.

The rise in Italy's economic standing (in GDP terms, Italy ranks behind Germany and France, but close to or above the UK) has given birth to a new nationalism. This performance has been achieved in the swing away from fascism since the Second World War.

Italy has a North/South divide, demarcated just south of Rome. Milan, in the industrialised North, is the centre of business and, according to Northern Italians, sophistication as well. The Southerners, with Neapolitans as a prime example, tend to be more relaxed in their outlook and less speedy in their business transactions. However, the volatile Italian temperament seems to transcend regional differences! The Italians use their whole bodies in communication, gesticulating widely with their arms and shoulders.

Punctuality is not a feature of Italian behaviour, but making unilateral decisions to change or cancel appointments is. When dealing with Italians it is you, not them, who must adjust to a different tempo and culture. They are easily offended and excited, but tend to have an impersonal approach to business. If quick decisions are required, expect to wait until the very last moment, and, if government departments are involved in your negotiations, allow plenty of time, since bureaucratic transactions take a very long time and patience is always necessary. Insistence can also be important: in the country of Machiavelli, much can be done to restrict the progression of unwanted, but officially allowable, decisions.

The young are the driving force in Italy, bringing the country into line with European trends. The word 'yuppie' has been incorporated into the vocabulary, and the consumer-spend mentality that category represents is an index of modern Italian society.

Italians are distinguished from other Europeans by the singular use of their language, coupled with their zest for life. Handshaking is extensively used and an attempt to speak and write their language is almost universally appreciated.

MAKING THE APPOINTMENT

Write early for an appointment and make sure, if possible, that the letter is in good Italian. In this initial communication, express the purpose of your meeting, giving as much detail as you can. You should allow your Italian counterpart time to respond to you and to make an appointment. However, Italians are not great letter-writers and, if you have not heard within three to four weeks of writing, then a telephone call to your contact's secretary will help.

The Italian's use of a secretary's skills varies. In large multinationals secretaries will be used to their full capacity; in smaller companies only their typing will be in demand. You will be able to identify in what capacity your particular counterpart's secretary acts by her ability to make the appointment on behalf of her boss. You may need to insist on speaking to him directly. Use facsimile if you are unable to make contact verbally.

Once the appointment is fixed, reconfirm a week or so before leaving home, and again the day before the meeting is due to take place. Italians move their diary appointments to suit themselves, and do not always feel the need to inform those who are not part of their day's plans. You should make sure that you are accompanied by those who have the skills to progress business matters; engineers, marketing men and interpreters. (You should offer in your letter to bring an interpreter, if necessary.) Be on time, and be patient.

THE MEETING

The volatile character of the Italians, together with their often impersonal approach to business, can make them difficult negotiating partners. Add to this the fact that they will usually be impeccably dressed, immaculately groomed, and work from well-appointed offices, and the prospect can be quite daunting.

In the first meeting much time will be spent in deciding whether the company wishes to do business with you. (In other words, they will be summing you up.) Go at the Italians' pace, oiling the wheels of communication with appropriate compliments. Italians are probably among the best at delivering a disparaging remark in the most charming way. Do not let them get away with this; respond with the same level of wit, eloquence and charm. Italians respect those who compete and win on their own terms. At all times, retain a calm exterior and do not react to any momentary change in your host's moods.

ENTERTAINING

Business meals

Italians are great lovers of good food, and will usually be happy for lunch or dinner to form part of the business transaction. Breakfast is a small meal in Italy, consisting of coffee and rolls. It is also taken early, and so makes a poor opportunity for business transactions. Working breakfasts are also perceived to be very American – not a positive attribute.

Lunch, on the other hand, will be costly in food and time. An invitation to lunch or dinner should be accepted; not to do so would be seen as ungracious. If you have more than one meeting during the morning, bear in mind Italian timekeeping and check out the prospects of business entertainment. The Italians are experts on food and enjoy opportunities for hospitality, so let them choose the restaurant and compliment them on the food served.

Wine will be plentiful, but your Italian colleague will not take offence if you do not drink at his pace; and if you cannot, you should not try!

Dinner appointments are offered less regularly than lunch, are taken at around 9.00 pm, and suggest progression in the negotiations. Initially, the meal is likely to be taken at a restaurant favoured by your counterpart, where his local presence will be recognised and commented upon. Whoever issued the invitation should offer to pay, but don't be surprised if Italians insist. A little resistance would be considered good manners, but give in gracefully and quickly. If you should be invited home to meet the family, this is a sign of good progress in your relationship. A small gift to the hostess is expected. This may be wine (make sure it is Italian, and recognisably good), flowers or chocolates. Small gifts for the children, if they are of an appropriate age, would be appreciated.

Subjects for social discussion

The Italians are very proud of their families, and complimenting them and enjoying their successes are good discussion topics. Overt pride in (but not comparison with) your own family is also very acceptable.

Business hospitality

As in most European countries, this is used much less than in the UK. Personally arranged events are a great deal more common. An invitation to spend some time at the summer house should, if at all possible, be accepted.

Gifts

Generosity is a national trait which Italians share with other Mediterranean countries. Gifts outside the business transaction might well be made and, if not seen as an immediate response, will be appreciated. The Italians like to give stylish gifts which have fairly high value, so make sure, if you are giving business gifts, that they represent the quality of your company.

Dress

Style emerges through all of the Italians' dealing, and their dress is no exception. The Italians are proud of their fashion designers and men are exceptionally well groomed on almost all occasions. Conservative, well-cut suits, shirts and ties should be chosen. It is acceptable to remove tie and jacket, but wait upon an invitation from your host or, if he is already so dressed, ask permission. If you are going to remove your designer jacket, make sure you are wearing a designer shirt, too! Women dress well, but not flamboyantly. Good shoes are an important part of an Italian's wardrobe.

WOMEN IN BUSINESS

Women are becoming more accepted in the service industries and commerce. There is still considerable male chauvinism, particularly in industrial companies and in the South. Italians will be charming, but expect to have a decision referred back to a male decision-maker. Women should not be surprised at this, and may have to ease their Italian colleagues into a new understanding.

WORKING HOURS AND PUBLIC HOLIDAYS

Business usually starts early, around 8.00–9.00 am, and a long break is taken at about one o'clock. Work recommences at about 4.00 pm, and continues into the early evening, finishing between 7.00 and 8.00 pm. The Italians enjoy their holidays which are, on average, four or five weeks, taken in one long break in the summer months, usually August. This will normally be spent with the extended family unit.

Public holidays are:

1st January	(New Year's Day)
25th April	Liberation Day)
1st May	(Labour Day)
15th August	(Assumption)
1st November	(All Saints' Day)
8th December	(Immaculate Conception)
25th December	(Christmas Day)
26th December	(St Stephen's Day)

There is, in addition, Easter Monday, which is movable.

LETTER-WRITING

The envelope

English	Italian
Mr	Egregio Signor (initials, surname), or Egr Sig* (initials, surname)
Mrs	Gentile Signora (initials, surname), or Gent ma Sig ra (initials, surname)
Miss	Gentile Signorina (initials, surname), or Gent ma Sig na (initials, surname)

Salutation

Italian	Letter written in: English
Egregio Signor (Surname)	Dear Mr (Surname), or Dear Signor (Surname)
Gentile Signora (Surname)	Dear Mrs (Surname), or Dear Signora (Surname)
Gentile Signorina	Dear Miss (Surname), or

(Surname)	Dear Signorina (Surname)
Egregio Signor	Dear Sir
Egregio Signori	Dear Sirs

Closing

Individual	Distinti Saluti, or La prego di gradire i miei piu cordiali saluti	Yours sincerely
Company	Distinti saluti	Yours faithfully

Note

*It is the custom to abbreviate titles, but only on the envelope. The first forename may be used in place of an initial.

MARKETING

The Italian media industry has recently undergone two major changes. The first is due to an upswing, since 1983, of the Italian economic climate, and the second was caused by wide-ranging government legislation. For instance, in the press sector since 1988 there is no longer fixed pricing for newspaper sales, and the government has stopped financially supporting the daily press.

Other changes include the improvement in distribution and a participation in the Europe-wide growth in magazine titles. Italian television is not known for its quality programming, but is famed for its 'stripping housewives'. It has over 350 local channels, but only three state-owned channels. Television is thought to have played an important part in unifying the country within its new national consciousness by highlighting the similarities of different regions rather than their differences.

Socio-economically, the country is broken down into four main segments:

Table 14.1   Socio-economic grading in Italy

	%
Upper/upper middle	10.7
Middle	46.9
Middle/lower	34.6
Lower	7.8

Source ISPI

The marketing spend is as follows:

Table 14.2   Marketing spend in Italy

	%
Newspapers	22.0
Magazines	19.2
TV	49.5
Radio	3.6
Cinema	0.3
Outdoor	5.4

Source ASSAP

The spend rankings by key categories are:

Table 14.3   Key categories spend in Italy

(1) Food
(2) Toiletries, healthcare
(3) Automotive
(4) Beverages
(5) Mass media
(6) Clothing and fabrics
(7) Household cleaners

Source NASA

Media

VAT is levied on all media at 18 per cent. Tobacco advertising is forbidden on all media. Alcoholic beverages and a large number of other products are subject to restrictions on state TV, whilst advertisements for the following are not allowed: contraceptives, weapons and accessories, products and treatments for physical development, gambling houses and horse-race betting halls, betting contests and lotteries (except those organised on behalf of public organisations), moneylenders and companies offering loans (except public banks or public financial institutions), fortune-tellers and the like, matrimonial agencies and correspondence clubs, employment agencies and bureaux, private investigation agencies, undertakers, entertainments restricted to adults and newspapers of political organisations.

Apart from tobacco advertising, independent TV has no

advertising restrictions. For further information, contact: SACIS, via Tomacelli 139, Rome (Tel: (+39) 639 6841).

CONSUMER PREFERENCES/DIFFERENCES

Household spend

The Italians are spending more on their home although their priority is still on the purchase of food rather than on household equipment and appliances. Indeed, they have one of the lowest spends on home electrical appliances.

The breakdown of household spending on domestic goods and services is as follows.

Table 14.4   Italian household spend

Items	%
Furniture (including carpets and other floor coverings)	28
White goods	12
Furnishings	9
Table utensils	6
Domestic and other household services	45

Source Eurostat/Mintel

Financial awareness

The Italians have a fairly low level of banking use. This trend is also followed in the penetration of credit cards, which is low.

Food spend

Food and drink play a large part in Italian life. The Italians consume more pasta and bread than any other country in the EU. They also have the highest percentage of consumption of fish per capita. Equal amounts of beef, veal, pork and poultry are eaten.

Italy is a wine producing nation and wine consumption is high, second only to that in France. Comparatively little beer is drunk.

General consumer spend

Of all the EU member states, the Italians have the most inward-looking regard to the purchase of their cars; for example, Fiat have over 60 per cent of the home market. The Italians have the second highest level of passenger car purchase in the EU.

The highest priority for the Italian single man is his preference for spending on clothes. As far as men's clothes are concerned the Italian male spends more money on his stylish looks than on his cars or motorcycles. This trend is not followed by the women although recently there has been an increase in their spending levels with regard to clothes.

Political trends

With a total of 81 Euro seats at stake, the Italian electorate proved that their interest in what happens in the EU was still very much alive. Italy recorded the third highest turnout of voters (82 per cent). The Green Party showed the most gain, winning five seats. This was their first election in Italy.

ESTABLISHING A BUSINESS

Foreign investors are free to adopt any of the forms of business entity available to Italian citizens. All companies and other entities established in Italy, even if by foreign investors, are governed by the Italian Civil Code, and there is no particular law concerning foreign investment. Special laws apply to banks, insurance companies, holding and trust companies. All new enterprises must register their establishment at the local court and Chamber of Commerce, notify the local tax office and, if staff are employed, register with the National Social Security Institute.

Companies that intend to import or export goods subject to licensing procedures must register with the Ministry of Foreign Trade, and all retailers (including suppliers of food and drink, mail order and vending machine operators) must be specially licensed by the municipal, or sometimes regional, authorities.

The minimum capital required for a *Società per Azioni (SpA)* – public (joint stock) company – is Lit 200,000,000. For a private (limited liability) company – *Società a responsabilità limitata (Srl)* – the minimum capital is Lit 20,000,000. The capital is represented by quotas, each having a minimum par value of Lit 1,000. Subscriptions can be made in cash and 'in kind'. 'Pay-in-kind' is restricted, and must be of property with an economic value.

Management structure

The governing bodies of a SpA are the shareholders in general meeting, the directors and the statutory auditors. Management is entrusted to a sole director or Board of Directors; the latter may contain both executives and independent members. The size of the Board is determined by the provisions of the company's Articles of Association. The chairman of the board must be elected by the directors or the shareholders; normally directors need not be Italian citizens or residents and they need not be shareholders. Directors are liable to the company for any failure to fulfil their duties, and may be liable to shareholders or third parties who are harmed by the director's actions, neglect or fraudulent behaviour.

There is a Board of Statutory Auditors (*Sindaci*) numbering some three or five persons; members are not required to be Italian citizens and must not be employees or directors (or close relatives of directors of the company.

According to the law, the statutory auditors are responsible for ensuring that the law and the articles of association are respected and the company's accounting records are properly kept. In addition, the statutory auditors are responsible for the quarterly checking of the company's cash in hand and the existence of investments, the examination and approval of the annual balance sheet, and the valuation of the company's assets.

As with a SpA, directors of an Srl have the power to represent and bind the company in business. Statutory audits do not apply unless the company's capital exceeds lira 100,000,000.

At present, there are no legal requirements to institute works councils, or to include employees' representatives on Boards of Directors. However, a workers' committee (*consiglio di fabbrica*) is usually established, the number of members of which depends on the size of the company concerned. This committee is entitled to information concerning the company's economic situation, sales, production and employment.

USEFUL ADDRESSES

Sources of information and help

Italian Chamber of Commerce for Great Britain
Walmer House
29b Regent Street
London W1X 6AE
Tel: 071-637 3062
Fax: 071-436 6037

British Chamber of Commerce for Italy
Via Agnello 8
I-20124 Milan
Tel: (+39) 2 876981
Tlx: 332490 BRITAL I

Research sources

AC Nielsen Company
Via Dante 7
I-20123 Milan
Tel: (+39) 2 85621
Tlx: 3340591

Doxa (member of the Gallup organisation)
Galleria San Carlo 6,
I-20122 Milan
Tel: (+39) 2 790871
Tlx: 335161 DOXA I

Addresses for advertisers

SACIS (for details of advertising legislation)
Via Tomacelli 139,
Rome
Tel: (+39) 6 396841

Italian Association of Advertising Agencies
19 via Larga
20122 Milan
Tel: (+39) 2802 086

*Associazione Italiana delle Agenzie di Pubblicita a Servicio
Completo* (advertising association)
Via Larga 19
I-20122 Milan
Tel: (+39) 02 802086

Chambers of Commerce

Florence   P dei Giudici 3
Florence
Tel: (+39) 55 27951

Genoa   Genoa Chamber of Commerce
Via Garibaldi 4
Genoa
Tel: (+39) 10 12094

Chamber of Commerce for Foreign Trade
P. Banchi
Genoa
Tel: (+39) 10 208864

Milan   Chamber of Commerce6p Affari
20123 Milan
Tel: (+39) 285151

Chamber of Commerce for International Exchange
Via 18 Gennaio
Milan
Tel: (+39) 2 2719288

International Chamber of Commerce
Via Cordusio 2
Milan
Tel: (+39) 2 802517

Naples   Naples Chamber of Commerce
P. Bovio
Naples
Tel: (+39) 81 207222

Chamber of Commerce for International Exchange
Via Flavio Gioia 4
Naples
Tel: (+39) 81 310347

Rome   Piazza di Pietra
00186 Roma
Tel: (+39) 6 570071

Turin   Via San Frencesco da Paola 24
Turin
Tel: (+39) 11 57161

Venice   Via XXII Marzo
2032 San Marco
Venice
Tel: (+39) 41 703499

Principal Euro Info Centres

Eurosportello
Via delle Orsole
I-20143 Milan
Tel: (+39) 2 154456

Eurosportello
4/b Corso Meridionale 58
I-80143 Naples
Tel: (+39) 81 269897

Eurosportello
Via Ciprol
I-25124 Brescia
Tel: (+39) 30 222172

Eurosportello
Via San Domenica 4
I-40124 Bologna
Tel: (+39) 51 529611

15
LUXEMBOURG

INTRODUCTION

The importance of Luxembourg as one of the founder countries of the EEC has little to do with its size or its population, which is the lowest of all the member states. Luxembourg, like many smaller countries of the European Union, has maintained its importance to the Community by using what resources it has to create a role for itself. For Luxembourg this derives from its geographical positioning. Quite literally, it is at the heart of Europe. Owing more to its German rather than French neighbours, it now has three official languages: French, German and Luxembourgish. French is the most popular language in use, and today the country is culturally more tied to France than to Germany.

In 1921 a convention of Economic Union was signed between Luxembourg and Belgium. This created a customs-free zone, and gave Luxembourg and Belgium fiscal parity with one another.

The small population (367,000) is supplemented by many foreign businesses, but the lack of a firm national character has led the Luxembourger to be somewhat distant and sensitive about his nation. For this reason, Luxembourgers jealously guard their separate identity, and should by no means be considered as vaguely French, German or Belgian. In general, Luxembourgers are friendly and like to show off their language skills; they appreciate attempts to use the Luxembourg dialect for simple greetings and thank-yous.

Luxembourg is not renowned for its exciting lifestyle, although this may change as it becomes recognised as the major European centre of banking and investment fund management. Luxembourg's prominence comes from its realistic taxation on investment income, and this is where it proposes to be at the centre of Europe in more ways than geographic.

MAKING THE APPOINTMENT

It is best, in the first instance, to send a letter to an organisation in Luxembourg in order to arrange a visit. English is well understood in commerce, but as French is the main language it would be wise to use French for the business transaction, provided you have a working knowledge of that language. Offers of an interpreter at any meeting would be well received, but may not always be necessary.

The role of the secretary is rather more formal also, but is more in the French style with large multinationals using all the secretarial skills and small businesses and professionals using just typing skills. Regardless of her immediate ability to help (she may not have the boss's diary), the secretary is to be won over and respected, as she can play an influential role in securing subsequent interviews.

THE MEETING

The European practice of handshaking is much in evidence in Luxembourg business practice. The business environment tends to be very formal, with addressing by surname retained for much longer than is usually the case elsewhere.

The first meeting will be held in the company's office and it is very important to be on time. As well as being formal in his outlook, the Luxembourger is fastidious in his business ways. Regardless of whether the business interview is with commerce or government (government offices stay open to 6.00 pm, commercial offices are open usually until 5.00 pm), expect a very traditional atmosphere, particularly if your business counterpart is over fifty. Here, old social structures of titles and appropriately-styled respect are still required to give a good impression.

ENTERTAINING

Business meals

The breakfast meeting is not very common in Luxembourg and lunch is by no means an automatic follow-on if the time is right.

Lunch is a sure sign of progression in the interview; it will be quite short and in a good quality restaurant but it is unlikely that you will be offered lunch at home. If you extend the invitation, let him choose the location and you pay. Entertaining can be very expensive. However, because of the small size of the country, business hospitality is not usually ostentatious and is most likely to take the form of dinner, with perhaps a visit to a nightclub afterwards.

Dinner is likely to be taken outside the family home, and only business associates will attend; even this is an important sign of the building of a successful rapport. If you should be invited to dinner at home, flowers should be taken for the lady of the house and a bottle of wine for the host is acceptable. At all times remain formal in your dealings; take your cue from your host as to when to become more relaxed.

Subjects for social discussion

So far as small talk is concerned, Luxembourgers are usually happy to talk about their families. They are especially proud of their cars which they see as highly prestigious.

An understanding of the history and culture of Luxembourg is much appreciated, as it confirms your recognition of the distinct status of their country. Very little corporate entertainment is done, except perhaps at the trade fair which is held twice yearly.

Luxembourg is a very European, and small, nation. It has boundaries with Belgium, France and Germany, and takes an interest in the current affairs of all these countries. However, Luxembourgers are proud of their own national identity and topics of discussion that relate to the development of their own language and culture are popular. Do not draw too many similarities, and in particular with Belgium.

Business hospitality

Because of the size of the country and its population, opportunities to be lavish are limited. As mentioned before, the more likely routes are the one-to-one meetings with relaxing dinners and night-clubs to follow.

Gifts

So far as business gifts are concerned, the acceptable practices of most Northern European Union states apply here. Gifts should not be too lavish.

Dress

Formality is best. It is expected that conservative suits, shirts and ties should be worn on most business occasions. For women, smart, conventional clothes are the norm; trousers should not be worn.

WOMEN IN BUSINESS

Women play an ever-increasing role in Luxembourg's business life. They are generally well-educated, but the growth of their role follows the slow path adopted by most Community states. However Luxembourg tends, on the whole, to be male-oriented and although women are encouraged to take part in business, there is a male chauvinism which permeates the business community. The employment of women is most widespread in the service industries.

WORKING HOURS AND PUBLIC HOLIDAYS

Normal working hours are between 8.30 am and 12.00 am in the morning, and 2.00–5.30 pm in the afternoon. On average, Luxembourgers have four weeks' annual holiday.

The following are public holidays:

1st January	(New Year's Day)
1st May	(Labour Day)
23rd June	(National Day)
15th August	(Assumption)
1st November	(All Saints' Day)
2nd November	(All Souls' Day)
25th/26th December	(Christmas Day)

In addition, there are four movable days, including Easter.

LETTER-WRITING

For a letter which is written in French see page 113; and for a letter in German see page 127.

MARKETING

The marketing infrastructure of Luxembourg is underdeveloped compared to the structure found in its Community partners. The following is a summary of its content.

At the present time there are no consumer media or sector spends available for comparison. There are, for instance, only 250,000 radios and 150,000 television sets in the whole of the Grand Duchy. *Radio-Tele Luxembourg* operates four radio and three TV stations, broadcasting nationally.

As far as newspapers are concerned, there are six daily newspapers, of which *Luxembourger Wort* or La Voix du Luxembourg (printed in German and French) are considered to be the main national papers. The French paper *Le Republicain Lorrain* has a large Luxembourg section and therefore has its own readership following.

CONSUMER PREFERENCES/DIFFERENCES

Very little data are available on the preferences of consumers in Luxembourg. Data are usually combined with those of the Belgian consumer. What does emerge is that Luxembourgers spend highly on their home, both furnishings and appliances. Clothes are also considered important with the more conservative of foreign designers selling well in that market.

The food consumption in Luxembourg ranks highly, *per capita*, with the rest of the community. Large quantities of pork in various forms, for example, sausages, ham, fresh meat, etc, are sold.

Harmonisation of car tax (VAT) could affect car sales as Luxembourg has one of the lowest levels of VAT (12 per cent) in the Community.

Political trends

The citizens of Luxembourg again showed how keenly aware they are of their role in selecting their representatives in Strasbourg. Luxembourg has the second highest turnout of voters in the EU showing 87 per cent. Of that, the Christian Democrats still hold three out of Luxembourg's total of six Euro seats.

ESTABLISHING A BUSINESS

Every commercial and industrial enterprise must obtain a government licence to trade. This licence will be granted only if the individual responsible produces certificates of good conduct and solvency and (with some exceptions) evidence of appropriate qualifications. These can be proved by submitting a relevant diploma or a certificate of practical experience in the trade concerned. The period of experience required varies from three months to three years. If the activity is to be exercised by a corporate body, these conditions must be fulfilled by the director or manager in charge.

A written application for a licence must be sent to the Ministry for Small and Medium-Sized Businesses, in the case of a commercial undertaking, or the Ministry of Economy, in the case of an industrial undertaking. Banks and insurance companies must obtain the approval of the Ministry of Finance.

There are two types of company: the *Société à Responsabilité Limitée (SARL)* – the private company; and *Société Anonyme (SA)* – the public company. Both are governed by the same legal framework, with the difference occurring in the type of shares issued and the capital requirements. For instance, SARLs do not have conventional shares, but '*parts sociales*' and the minimum capitalisation is LF 100,000, whereas SAs have a full range of share options and a minimum capitalisation of LF 1,250,000.

Within one month of starting up, every enterprise must register basic information concerning itself, such as constitution documents and names of directors, managers and statutory auditors, with the *Administration de l'Enregistrement et des Domaines*, and file this information in the Register of Commerce (*Registre de Commerce*) kept at the District Court for the area in which the legal address of the enterprise is located. The Register of Commerce provides a copy for publication in the Official Gazette. Any changes in this information must be registered and filed in the same way, within one month of the change. Small filing fees are payable.

Every business entity is required to join the Chamber of Commerce, to which a subscription, based on profit, is payable. Enterprises having an activity subject to VAT must inform the appropriate office of the *Administration de l'Enregistrement*. The authorities collecting direct taxes such as income tax and municipal business tax must be informed, as must the Social Security Office.

Management structure

Management of the corporation is vested in a board of directors consisting of at least three members (nine, if employees can appoint directors to represent them). The directors need not be Luxembourg citizens or residents, or shareholders of the corporation.

The Board of Directors is responsible for the management of the corporation, although day-to-day management can be delegated to one or several directors or managers.

If an SA company employs at least 1,000 persons (and in some other special cases), one-third of its directors must be designated by the employees, including manual workers. The conditions of all directors' appointments, discharges and duties are determined by the articles of association, whether the directors are appointed by shareholders or employees.

Any SA employing at least 150 persons must set up a works council (*comité mixte d'entreprise*) composed of an equal number of management representatives and employees' representatives. The works council participates in decisions concerning welfare, health and safety, employee selection and evaluation and similar matters. It has the right to be informed and consulted on working conditions and significant economic matters. If the SA has 15 or more employees, then it must have employee delegates (*délégations du personnel*). These delegates hold at least six meetings per year, three of which are with the management. Delegates can only be dismissed in exceptional circumstances.

USEFUL ADDRESSES

Chamber of Commerce

Luxembourg
7 rue Alcide de Gaspert
Luxembourg
L-2981 Kirchberg
BP 1503
Tel: (+352) 43 58 53

Radio-Tele Luxembourg (RTL)
Villa Lowulguy
PO Box 1002 2850
Tel: (+352) 47601

Principal Euro Info Centre

Euroguichet
7 rue Alcide de Gaspert
BP 1503
L-2981 Kirchberg
Luxembourg
Tel: (+352) 43 58 53

16
THE NETHERLANDS

INTRODUCTION

The Dutch, the middle-men of Europe, long ago established themselves as excellent traders, good negotiators and financially sound businesspeople. They have a commercial relationship with the UK dating back before the sixteenth century. Indeed, the first Anglo-Dutch Chamber of Commerce was set up in 1891. The Dutch also share similar tastes and attitudes with the British.

The Dutch business acumen is evident in its major international organisations; companies such as Philips, Shell and Unilever. Carrying the Community's stereotyping of thriftiness and ruthlessness in business, the Dutch have perhaps contributed more to the spirit of a united Europe than any other member nation.

Dutch society mirrors Britain to some extent, since it has a royal family and a Parliament – though the Dutch Parliament is elected by proportional representation. Like most nations, the Dutch are proud of their history and cultural achievements; unlike most, however, they have developed the ethos of foreign language, and as well as their native Dutch (little-used elsewhere in the world) most businesspeople speak English and at least one other European language – most likely French or German. The Dutch mastery of foreign languages is well proven by the following table:

Table 16.1   Mastery of language

Country	Total speaking at least one language	one language	Speaking at least two languages	three languages
	%	%	%	%
Netherlands	70.7	28.7	31.7	10.3
Belgium	43.6	22.4	15.5	5.7
Germany	39.5	32.8	6.0	0.7
France	32.6	26.0	6.0	0.7
UK	25.4	20.0	4.7	0.7

Figures produced by the World Economic Forum also rank the Netherlands high in terms of the country's political stability and successful labour relations.

To summarise a recent Netherlands Chamber of Commerce report:

> '1992 will not harmonise cultural aspects. Europe will remain fragmented regarding: language, taste, attitudes and business practice. It is here that the Dutch will benefit from the skills of international marketing and sales, transport and distribution.'

A further advantage for the Dutch is that they can reach any of the major economic centres in Europe within one day's surface travel.

MAKING THE APPOINTMENT

In all dealings with the Dutch, your overriding concerns must be punctuality, straightforwardness and lack of pretension. The Dutch Chamber of Commerce takes a leading role in making contacts in the Netherlands and should be used for the initial contact.

Once given a name, it is acceptable to telephone. The telephone call for an appointment should be confirmed by a letter. This should be concise, informative and provide all the information the Dutch counterpart will need to join you in discussions. Write to the person you wish to see, and by name; not to do so is considered very rude.

The secretary's role is similar to that in the UK: the larger the company, the more likely she is to hold the diary and be aware of the importance of your visit. She and your counterpart should be addressed with the maximum, at least initially, of formality and British good manners.

The content of your letter should always offer an interpreter by way of admission of lack of linguistic skill in Dutch (usually rejected because of the large number of English-speaking executives) and information about any advisers attending. Do not turn up with advisers unexpectedly, as this tactic may well antagonise your counterpart and so remove any advantage you may have gained.

THE MEETING

The Dutch way of conducting business will mean first, that if he agrees to see you he is 'interested' in your proposal and second that the meeting will be quite short (maximum 30–45 minutes). This would equate to an hour or an hour-and-a-half meeting in the UK.

An important cultural point to check when dealing is the use of numbers in Dutch. The Dutch speak the units first and the tens second; even if they speak English well, this may lead to some confusion. For instance, 98,000 spoken by your Dutch counterpart could mean 89,000 to your partner. Check in writing before concluding the deal.

Do not be late for the meeting, and use your business card; this is very important to the Dutch. Small talk is acceptable in the meeting. The Dutch are proud of their houses, offices and cars and these are personally important to them. In your presentations, do not understate your case or achievements (a British phenomenon!); the Dutch will view this either as a lack of commitment or take it literally. At all times, be direct and honest in your business affairs. The Dutch will be good partners except when you don't deliver. No delivery is the supplier's fault, regardless of the reason. The Dutch are more likely to stop doing business with you for not fulfilling a delivery date (within reason) than to sue you.

The Dutch are very good negotiators and can be a trifle ruthless. They tend not to be particularly nationalistic, but it does pay to introduce yourself in Dutch, to have some knowledge of the Dutch royal family and ministers, and to understand something of the Dutch culture. It is also important to avoid calling their country Holland, which in fact refers only to a couple of the provinces and not to the whole of the country.

ENTERTAINING

Business meals

Lunch in the Netherlands is taken fairly early; between 12.30 pm and 1.30 pm. If you are not invited do not take this as a slight, it is not negative reaction; to be invited is a positive indicator in your favour. The Dutch hate pretension (and remember their thriftiness!), so lunch is unlikely to be elaborate; more likely a beer and a sandwich. Whoever issues the invitation, pays the bill.

Breakfast meetings are not common, but dinner is a more relaxed affair. Business is generally not conducted over dinner. Formal entertainment of the 'sponsorship' type is not common in the Netherlands, but informal arrangements are.

If you are invited to your host's home, do not take wine:

flowers or chocolate for the hostess are expected. Because of
the Netherland's flower industry, you should spend approximately £8 to £10 on flowers for the 'right' sized bunch.
Greetings are formal; handshaking is important and, when
meeting the hostess, should be offered. More familiar associates
will kiss cheek-to-cheek; do not do it, wait for the hostess to
offer. A letter of thanks for hospitality is always welcome, as is
the offer of reciprocal entertainment in your home.

Subjects for social discussion

The Dutch are well informed on British news. They are major
trading partners with the UK, with nearly 15 per cent of their
exports going into Britain. Because they receive BBC television,
they are as up-to-date as most Britons on British current affairs.
The restricted use of their language internationally requires
that they maintain a wide European perspective. The Dutch
enjoy their business success and are usually happy to discuss
business-related topics. Sport, especially football, Dutch culture
and family life are safe subjects. The Dutch sense of humour is
very similar to the British.

Business hospitality

The Dutch are not exhibitionists, and thus business hospitality
is unlikely to include lavish corporate events. Personal
invitations are given more out of genuine personal friendship
than out of corporate ambition.

Gifts

Only business-type brand gifts are usual. These should not be
ostentatious, and certainly will not help in shaping the
business deal.

Dress

Well-dressed and semi-formal is the key to business dressing in
the Netherlands. Blazer and slacks are acceptable for men,
although suits are safest, with smart ties and shirts. Ties are
retained at all times. Women have greater flexibility, but should
always remain smart.

WOMEN IN BUSINESS

Women have open access to business, but still form a small
percentage of senior managers.

WORKING HOURS AND PUBLIC HOLIDAYS

The core working time in the Netherlands is 9.00 am to 5.30 pm, but younger executives will usually add an hour on either side of these times. After work, they are likely to go straight home but will, unlike the Germans, expect to take work home with them. Telephone calls outside office hours will be welcomed, provided there is a real urgency about the business message.

On average, the Dutch have four weeks' holiday a year, which is split into two holidays: a winter sports, and a longer summer holiday. The summer season, between mid-July to mid-August is to be avoided.

1st January	(New Year's Day)
30th April	(Queen's Birthday)
25th/26th December	(Christmas Day)

In addition, there are four movable days, including Good Friday and Easter Monday.

LETTER-WRITING

The envelope

Dutch	English
De Heer (initials, surname)	Mr
Mevrouw (initials, surname)	Mrs
Mejuffrouw (initials, surname)	Miss

Salutation

Dutch	Letter written in: English
Geachte Heer (surname)	Dear Mr (surname)
Geachte Mevrouw (surname)	Dear Mrs (surname)
Geachte Mejuffrouw (surname)	Dear Miss (surname)
Geachte Heer/Geachte Mevrouw	Dear Sir, Dear Madam
Mijne Heren	Dear Sirs

Closing

| Individual | Hoogachtend (or less (formally) met vriendelyke groeten hoogachtend | Yours sincerely |
| Company | Hoogachtend | Yours faithfully |

Note
Initials only are used, not forenames. Letters (eg for professional qualifications) are used after the surname, but only on the envelope. A person's business card is generally a good indicator of how they like to be addressed. Except at senior level, it is usual to write to the department concerned and not to the individual.

MARKETING

Advertising expenditure has a higher growth rate than GNP with 8.4 per cent growth in 1986 over 1985. The most significant element in the budget, compared with other countries, is direct advertising which, together with sales promotion, sponsorship and public relations, claims up to two-thirds of the advertising expenditure.

Satellite and cable television are matched by three Dutch television channels, forging a sophisticated board and narrow-cost media framework. New magazines and the re-emergence of posters complete the picture.

Consumers are classified in a similar manner to the UK, but with classification 'B' split, rather than 'C'.

Table 16.2   Consumer classification in percentage of population in the Netherlands

Socio-economic class	%
A	16
B_1/B_2	29
C	39
D	16

Source Summo Scanner, 1987

The media spend is divided in the following way:

Table 16.3 Media spend in the Netherlands

	%
Newspapers	34
Magazines	11
TV	5
Skychannel	1
Radio	1
Outdoors (including sports sponsorship)	4
Direct advertising	44

Source VEA

The spend rankings by key categories are:

Table 16.4 Key categories spend rankings in the Netherlands

(1) Banks, insurance, finance
(2) Cars, motorcycles
(3) Food
(4) Travel
(5) Alcoholic drinks
(6) Radios, TVs, record players
(7) Household cleaners
(8) Tobacco

Source Bureau voor Budgellen Controle (BBC)

Media

There is no specific advertising tax. VAT is levied at 20 per cent on all media with the exception of press media published four or more times a year, for which the rate is 6 per cent. Certain restrictions are placed on advertisements for tobacco and cigarettes, alcoholic drinks, medicinal products and treatments, direct marketing, consumer credit loans, investment, property and sweets. No tobacco products may be advertised on TV. As from 1 January 1988, responsibility for compiling and supervising the rules and regulations on advertising in all media, including radio and TV, now rests with *De Stichting Reclame Code*. Westermarkt 2, 1016 DK Amsterdam (Tel: (+31) 20 257690/257721).

There are 49 daily titles, with a total daily circulation of 4.5 million copies and an average reach of 8.1 million persons (aged fifteen and over). Many of the leading dailies have local editions, and some publish colour supplements. The newspaper market, as far as dailies are concerned, is currently stable. Of the non-dailies (which include weeklies and papers published twice and three times a week) 129 belong to the *Nederslandse Nieuwsblad Pers*, which does not account for all non-dailies in existence. Over 700 free-sheets are published, with a total estimated circulation of six million copies. There are no Sunday papers in the Netherlands. The country offers a wide selection of magazines; however, not all of these carry advertising.

CONSUMER PREFERENCES/DIFFERENCES

Household spend

The Dutch have a lot in common with their Northern European neighbours, spending a high proportion of their money on furniture for the home. The same applies to household equipment, for example, more fridges are sold in the Netherlands than in any other member state.

Interestingly, the Dutch consumer, unlike the Italians or French, does not rank his first purchase consideration to be a home produced product. Quality and price are foremost considerations.

The breakdown of household spend on goods and services is as follows.

Table 16.5   Household spend in the Netherlands

Items	%
Furniture (including carpets and other floor coverings)	40
White goods	12
Furnishings	8
Table utensils	14
Domestic and other household services	26

Source Eurostat/Mintel

Financial awareness

Although they have the second largest options exchange in the world based in Amsterdam, the Dutch do not follow the Northern European trend of being financially aware. Fewer bank accounts are held in the Netherlands than in any other Northern European country. Their personal financial profile is more similar to that found in Mediterranean countries. This trend could change after 1992.

Food spend

Unlike their neighbours in Germany, the Dutch food spend is concentrated more on fresh produce rather than on tinned or frozen items. Beer and wine is consumed but not in any great volume.

The Dutch drink a considerable volume of coffee, second only to the Germans.

General consumer spend

The Dutch have one of the lowest rates of motorcycle ownership in the Community but the highest ownership of stereos.

As mentioned previously, they have little preference for purchasing durables, cars etc made in their own country. Given an increase in their spending power they would prefer a meal out than doing DIY!

Political trends

The Christian Democrats Party still retains popular support throughout the Netherlands, holding two-fifths of the Netherland's Euro seats.

However, voter awareness of the Euro elections is well below that of its neighbours, showing a 47 per cent turnout.

Green issues are still presented by the Rainbow Party: the number of seats won in 1989 remained at two, showing that green issues were holding.

ESTABLISHING A BUSINESS

The position of a foreign-owned company in the Netherlands is essentially the same as that of a Dutch-owned company. All new entities must comply with registration rules and meet various environmental and business requirements.

Every new business must be registered with the Trade Register of the Chamber of Commerce in the area in which it is located. Appointments of trade agents who have full powers of attorney to deal on behalf of foreign principals must also be registered.

The information to be filed in the register includes:

1. A copy of the articles of incorporation of the enterprise, including its name, its trade name, if different, its objectives and its registered address.
2. The amounts of authorised, issued and paid-in capital, and the names and addresses of any shareholders who have not fully paid in the capital contributions on their shares.
3. The names and personal particulars of the supervisory and managing directors.
4. The powers of each managing director.

Other requirements, including permits and formalities to be dealt with, are those arising from:

1. The Public Nuisance Act: this Act requires a licence to be obtained from the municipal authorities if any dangerous or disagreeable trade is to be carried on.
2. The Pollution of Surface Waters Act and the Air Pollution Act.
3. Other laws such as building regulations, the Factories Act, and the Shops Act.

Every new enterprise must also register with the office of direct taxation, indirect taxation (the VAT inspectorate) and social security.

An existing enterprise that already possesses all the necessary permits and licences, but is then acquired by foreigners, does not need to renew those permits and licences.

There are no requirements for Dutch participation in either the equity captial of a business entity or in its management. There are two types of limited liability company: the smaller *Besloten Vennootschap (BV)* private company, and the larger *Naamloze Vennootschap (NV)*. The legal requirements are very similar, but they differ in capitalisation and the nature of shares.

The minimum capital for a BV is DF 40,000 and for a NV DF 100,000. The BV can only have registered shares and cannot issue share certificates, whereas the NV can issue registered or bearer shares.

Management structure

Every company must have a managing director, or a management board with any appropriate number of members. In addition, a large company must have a supervisory board, consisting of at least three individuals. A 'large company' for this purpose is one:

1. with issued capital and consolidated reserves of DF 22.5 million or more;
2. which has established a works council (either itself or in a subsidiary company);
3. which, together with its subsidiary companies (if any), has 100 or more employees in the Netherlands.

The same rules apply to BV and NV companies.

In a large company (whether BV or NV), the supervisory board is solely responsible for appointing and dismissing the members of the management board, finalising the annual financial statements, and approving a number of major management decisions.

Shareholders, works councils and the management board itself are, however, entitled to nominate candidates for the supervisory board; the first two of these groups have a limited right of veto over proposed appointments by the supervisory board, although this right is exercised only in very exceptional circumstances.

In subsidiaries of foreign parent companies, even if these subsidiaries qualify as large companies, the authority to appoint and dismiss members of the management board and to finalise the annual financial statements may under certain conditions be reserved for the shareholders.

A smaller company may also institute a supervisory board in certain circumstances if it so decides, setting out the board's powers and duties in its articles of incorporation. Normally in such a case, the members of both boards are appointed and dismissed by the shareholders. Supervisory board members are not allowed to be executives or employees of the company; their function is to advise and supervise the company's management.

Every company with 100 or more employees who work more than one-third of normal working hours, must set up a works council made up by its employees. This council must be given, on demand, all the information it needs to perform its duties. In general, the council must be consulted on matters such as mergers, the set-up or closure of a business and important changes in the company's organisation, and must give its consent to proposals on employment policies, the hiring and training of personnel, safety regulations, etc. In companies with less than 100 employees, works councils' rights are slightly reduced.

Employees have no legal rights to elect members directly to either the supervisory or the management board. The works council must, however, be consulted on proposed nominations to the management board. Moreover, in large companies (as already defined) the works council is entitled to propose candidates for the supervisory board and object to nominations to that board.

Companies with 10–34 employees must enable the labour force to debate twice-yearly with the management board all important matters concerning the company.

USEFUL ADDRESSES

Sources of information and help

Netherlands-British Chamber of Commerce
The Dutch House
307-308 High Holborn
London WC1V 7LS
Tel: 071-405 1358
Fax: 071-405 1689

Netherlands-British Chamber of Commerce
Holland Trade House
Bezuidenhoutseweg 181
2594 AH
The Hague
Tel: (31) 70 47 8881
Tlx: 33122

Research sources

AC Nielsen Company
Amsteldijk 166
1079 LH
1085 Amsterdam
Tel: (+31) 20 444972
Tlx: 112659

Orange Nassaulaan 25 (qualitative research specialists)
P O Box 1075
AJ Amsterdam
Tel: (+31) 20 750071

Addresses for advertisers

The Netherland Association of Recognised Advertising Consultants (VEA)
(advertising agency)
A J Ernststraat 169
1085-Amsterdam
Tel: (+31) 20 425642

The European Society for Opinion and Marketing Research
J J Viottaastraat 29
1071 JP
Amsterdam
Tel: (+31) 20 642141

Chamber of Commerce

Amsterdam   24 Koningin Wilhelminaplein 13
Amsterdam
Tel: (+31) 20 176931

The Hague   Alexander Gogelweg 16
The Hague
Tel: (+31) 70 614101
Rotterdam
Coolsingel 58
Rotterdam
Tel: (+31) 10 145022

Principal Euro Info Centres

EG-Adviescentrum voor Ondernemigen
9 Dalstandreef/BP 112
NL-1112 XC Dremen-Zuid
Tel: (+31) 20 90 10 71

EG-Adviescentrum voor Ondernemigen
Prins Henenklaan Zlu
Postbus 955
NL-5700 AZ Helmond
Tel: (+31) 49 20 48 468

17
PORTUGAL

INTRODUCTION

The Portuguese, although inhabitants of part of the same peninsula as Spain, are quite a different nation from the Spanish. They maintain the Mediterranean pride of the Spanish, but couple it more with humanity than arrogance. It is worth remembering that, like the Dutch, the Portuguese were a strong trading nation and as such have close ties with some European partners. Although outsiders may couple the Spanish and Portuguese together in their minds, the Anglo-Portuguese relationship, for example, is longer in duration than any trading similarities there may be between the two Iberian nations.

Portugal is the poorest country in the EU. These economic facts have done nothing to dampen the Portuguese's pride in their past or the hospitality and downright friendliness of the people.

Their most recent history is dominated by the 1974 revolution, which is of similar sensitivity in discussion as Franco's Spain. Power, although now spread more equally owing to democracy, is, in business, still vested in 13 core families.

The country has no traditional North/South divide; there are the tourist centres of the Algarve, and then there is the rest of the country. There are two major business centres: Lisbon, and the more industrial Oporto.

Generally, the Portuguese expect much to come from their membership of the EU; they understand Portugal's lower production costs and wish to exploit them. The country's infrastructure is still struggling to match the revolutionary awakening of the country and, although education is valued, it is given by the state in two shifts: 8.00 am–12.30 pm, and 1.30–6.00 pm. The rich still retain a grip on the economy of the country, through their domination of the better private education system.

MAKING THE APPOINTMENT

A personal introduction is probably the best way of beginning a business relationship. If this is not possible, however, a letter is the next best approach. It can be in your own language; the Portuguese will not be offended by you not using their language, although they will be pleased if you do. The offer of an interpreter will also be welcomed. However, the likelihood of a written response is low. A telephone call within a week of your expected interview to confirm it would be wise.

The letter and telephone call should be directed to the head of the company, who will be willing and able to talk to you directly. The need to be protected from outsiders is of little interest to the Portuguese; the role of the secretary, therefore, is less significant than, say, in the UK. They are more likely to be a typist and message-taker.

THE MEETING

You should arrive on time for the meeting, but do be prepared to wait – two hours is not unusual. It is a brave person, however, who is willing to gamble and arrive late for a meeting with the Portuguese. Once the meeting is under way, discussion will be friendly and probably protracted, although the tone of the meeting will still remain quite formal after the initial hand-shaking. However, you will probably not get down to business straight away, so be prepared for some small talk and take the lead from your host. (Football and the beauty of Portugal are useful topics of conversation.)

Unlike most European countries, the qualification of a first degree also allows the use of the title 'Doctor'. You need to recognise that this title does not have the implications which pertain to it in other countries, but it is still polite to use it where appropriate.

The discussion will naturally lead to a business meal, where the final deal may be agreed. The Portuguese will agree in principle to the deal and then bring in their lawyers to finalise it. The deal will be honoured very much in the French style. The Portuguese tend to find it difficult to understand the importance of delivery dates. They will be hard to pin down, and surprised at the concern you show at a few days' or weeks' delay. Be prepared for a strong insistence on price; almost everything else is negotiable except the price to be paid. They will walk away from a deal rather than negotiate. In general, the Portuguese view the British as by far the most effective and efficient nation in the Community.

ENTERTAINING

Business meals

The Portuguese business day is weighted towards the evening. Breakfast meetings are unusual, but may be taken at nine or ten o'clock. Lunch is much more likely to be taken as a business extension. They will not drink excessively at lunch; one or two bottles of wine is usual, but they will not be offended if you do not drink or try to keep up. Lunch is likely to last for about two hours.

Dinner is also seen as an extension of the business day and an invitation to dinner, normally taken away from the home, is of no great significance (nor, in fact, is having dinner at your counterpart's home). If dinner is taken out, it is unlikely that your counterpart's wife will be invited. You should not press for this, even if you have dined at his home on previous occasions.

Take care to compliment the food, as this is very important to the Portuguese. Do not be surprised at the frequency of their smoking, and do not order Mateus Rosé. If you have extended the invitation, then you may offer to pay the bill but you should not insist as it is unlikely that you will succeed.

If you are entertained at home, flowers and chocolates are acceptable gifts, but make sure that red carnations are not included in any bouquet (they are the emblem of the revolution).

As a foreigner, you will find the hospitality extremely generous. It is quite possible, after only a short business relationship, to be invited away for the weekend with the family to their holiday home. A note of gratitude is well received, and should be sent within a couple of days of the trip. There is little in the way of formal business 'sponsorship' entertaining.

Subjects for social discussion

In general discussion, sport, the family and home are important, cars less so. Cultural history is also very important and images of the Portuguese equivalent of Shakespeare, Luis de Camoes, are currently used in many product promotions.

Business hospitality

It is very unlikely that corporate entertainment facilities will be available or offered, except by the major multinational companies. In general, business hospitality is conducted at a very personal level.

Gifts

Business gifts are restricted to small, acceptable items, perhaps with the company logo. The issue of 'generous' gifts to those who helped secure business is much less common today than in the past, although misappropriation of funds is not unknown.

Dress

Smart but informal dress is acceptable, although at the initial business meeting it would be prudent to stick to the conservative, lightweight business suit. Women should wear classic, feminine styles.

WOMEN IN BUSINESS

Few women are found in business in Portugal. Women tend to be regarded very much as wives and mothers first. The growth in education is helping to develop a better role for women in business, but, as in Greece, attitudes are changing very slowly.

WORKING HOURS AND PUBLIC HOLIDAYS

The normal office hours are 9.00 am–5.00 pm in Lisbon; in Oporto, factories will start an hour earlier. Out of office meetings will begin any time after 7.00 pm. It is not unusual for any of the professions to be working until midnight (an 11.30 dental appointment could well be in the evening). Business calls at home up until that time are the norm, and you should expect to receive them yourself. August is the month when most holidays are taken, and it is very difficult to do business during that time.

Public holidays are:

1st January	(New Year's Day)
25th April	(National Day)
1st May	(Labour Day)
10th June	(Camoes' Day)
13th June	(St Anthony's Day [Lisbon])
24th June	(St John's Day [Oporto])
15th August	(Assumption)
5th October	(Republic Day)
1st November	(All Saints' Day)
1st December	(Restoration Day)
8th December	(Immaculate Conception)
25th December	(Christmas Day)

There are, in addition, two movable days, including Good Friday.

LETTER-WRITING

The envelope

Portuguese	English
Exm° Senhor (forenames, surname)	Mr
Exmª Senhora D. (forenames, surname)	Mrs
Not used in business letters	Miss

Salutation

Portuguese	Letter written in: English
Exm^ad Senhor (forenames, surname)	Dear Mr (surname) or Dear Senhor (surname)
Exmª Senhora D. (surname)	Dear Mrs (surname) or Dear Senhora D. (surname)
Exm° Senhor, Exmª Senhora	Dear Sir, Dear Madam
Exm°s Senhores	Dear Sirs

Closing
Individual

Com os melhores cumprimentos, subscrevemo-me De V.Exª Atentamente	Yours sincerely

Company

Com os melhores cumprimentos, subscrevemo-nos, De V.Exª Atentamente	Yours faithfully

When sending a letter bear in mind the following points:

- Always use full forenames rather than initials on the envelope, and in the salutation, unless there are more than four.

- A wife can choose whether or not to take her husband's surname. If so, it is added to her existing family name. Men have just their family name.
- In business, address Miss as Mrs.
- If writing to a person one knows, it is usual to substitute 'Caro' for Exm^o Senhor, followed by the forenames and surname.

MARKETING

The advertising market in Portugal is booming. This is due to a growth in business through Portugal's membership of the European Union. This has led to big, international accounts being lined up with international agencies, and so these agencies are becoming more important than local agencies. The growth rate in advertising spending of 1987 over 1986 was 50 per cent. Although this has now slowed down a little, it gives some idea of the potential.

The country's consumers have been classified in a similar way to the UK, and are weighted in the following way:

Table 17.1   Consumer classification in Portugal

	%
AB	5
C_1	31
C_2	57
D	7

Source Quantum, Lisbon

The advertising spend is as follows:

Table 17.2   Media spend in Portugal

	%
Press	26
TV	54
Radio	13
Cinema	2
Outdoor	5

Source Sabatina

The spend rankings by key categories are:

Table 17.3   Key categories spend in Portugal

(1) Food
(2) Alcoholic beverages
(3) Other beverages
(4) Automotive
(5) Publishing
(6) Lotteries

Source Sabatina

Media

VAT is charged at 16 per cent. Taxes are liable on advertisements placed on TV at a rate of 2 per cent, radio at 3 per cent, cinema at 2 per cent, daily newspapers at 1 per cent while all other print media are liable to a 16 per cent advertisement tax. On outdoor advertising there is a levy of Esc 20 per square metre per month, with a discount on bookings of 10 square metres and above. No tobacco advertising is allowed except on outdoor media for a six-month period following the launch of a new brand. Alcoholic drinks may be advertised on TV and radio after 10.00 pm, but the advertisement may not show a person drinking. There are no restrictions on alcohol advertisement, in print or outdoor. All pharmaceutical product advertising must be approved by the relevant health authority. For further information contact: Portuguese Association of Advertising Agencies, Rua Rodrigo da Fonseca, 20–4, 4–DTO, 1000 Lisbon (Tel: (+351) 1 656518).

CONSUMER PREFERENCES/DIFFERENCES

Few statistics are available on the consumer habits in Portugal. What does emerge is noted below.

Household spend

In Portugal, there are low levels of ownership in electric appliances, this is not only true on the household appliance level but also for personal computers etc. However, per capita, Portugal has more stoves than its Iberian neighbour. As Portugal's wealth increases so will her demand for consumer/household items.

This is not to say that the statistics indicate that the

Portuguese spend very little on their homes. They do spend on their homes but because of the low level of income they remain at the bottom of the consumer spend table.

Financial awareness

Although most international banks have a presence in Lisbon and the major tourist centres, the use of banks and other financial institutions is limited. The same applies for credit cards.

Food spend

The Portuguese eat more poultry than any other meat; however, they have the lowest *per capita* spend on meat in the Community.

General consumer spend

The Portuguese are at the bottom of the EC league spend table when it comes to dressing themselves. Indeed, on average, the men spend more on their beer and wine than on their clothes. This is despite having a growing clothes manufacturing industry.

Political trends

The Socialist Party gained one seat although they were still in second place to the Christian Democrats. Out of a total of 24 Euro seats, 51 per cent of Portuguese voters turned out to elect their representatives.

ESTABLISHING A BUSINESS

Every new enterprise must register with the Commercial Register and the tax division of the Ministry of Finance. Most businesses are required to join an employers' guild and pay an annual fee to cover guild expenses. All investments must comply with health, security and environmental protection regulations. Investors planning large development projects are required to prepare a report on the likely ecological impact, for approval by the State Secretary for the Environment, before operations may commence. Industrial buildings must conform to standards established by the Ministry of Industry for the relevant sector, for example, concerning the distance between buildings.

The Portuguese legislation was rationalised in the 1986

Code, which incorporated the various and appropriate EC directives. This provided for four types of company formation:

1. The private limited liability or 'quota' company: *Sociedades por Quotas de Responsabilidade Limitada (Lda)*.
2. The corporation: *Sociedade Anonima de Responsabilidade Limitada (SA)*.
3. A partnership: *Sociedade en Nome Colectivo (SNC)*.
4. Two types of limited partnership.

The Lda is usually for smaller companies where the public capital is not required. An SA, however, is more complex, allowing the attraction of public money on the Stock Exchange.

An Lda minimum capitalisation is Esc 400,000, and each quota must have a minimum value of Esc 250. The minimum capital required for *Sociedade Anomina* is Esc 5,000,000, represented by shares with par value of no less than Esc 1,000.

Management structure

The management structure of an SA can be two- or three-tier. The two-tier structure has a Board of Directors (*Conselho de Administraçao*) and a Board of Auditors (*Conselho Fiscal*), whilst the three-tier consists of a directorate (*Direcçao*), the general board (*Conselho Geral*) and a statutory auditor (*Revisor Oficial de Contas*). Both structures have to be agreed in advance. The three-tier structure is the more modern.

In the traditional two-tier company, the Board of Directors undertakes the general management and the Board of Auditors has the role of supervising the company. Direct representation from the shareholders sit on the Board of Auditors. In the newer, three-tier form, the Directorate is composed of an uneven number of no more than five directors. The directors are normally appointed by the General Council. The Council cannot consist of more than 15 people, elected at a general shareholders' meeting, and its duties include electing and removing the directors, reviewing the supervisory actions of the directorate and verifying the corporation financial statements. Finally, there is the Statutory Auditor who must be a shareholder and who is appointed to examine the company accounts.

A 'quota' company is managed by one or more managers appointed by the members. A manager need not be a Portuguese national or resident. A member of the company may become a manager. A quota company, unlike an SA, is not required by law to have a Board of Auditors.

The law does not require workers' representatives to be included on the board of managers. However, workers' committees with three to eleven members, depending on the size of the company concerned, must be established. These committees must be given information, including financial information, but may not participate in corporate management.

USEFUL ADDRESSES

Sources of information and help

Portuguese Chamber of Commerce and Industry in the UK
4th Floor
New Bond Street House
1–5 New Bond Street
London W1Y 9PE
Tel: 071-493 9973
Fax: 071-493 4772

British–Portuguese Chamber of Commerce
Rua da Estrella 8
P-1200 Lisbon
Tel: (+351) 1 661586
Tlx: 12787 BRICHA P

Research sources

A C Nielsen Company (continuous retail audits)
Rua Rosa Aranjo 34.4
P-1200 Lisbon
Tel: (+351) 1 554412
Tlx: 12748

Addresses for advertisers

Portuguese Association of Advertising Agencies
Rua Rodrigo da Fonseca 20–4
4-DTO
1000 Lisbon
Tel: (+351) 1 654 672

Chambers of Commerce

Lisbon   89 Portas de S Antao
                       Lisbon

Oporto   Palacio da Bolsa
                      Oporto
                      Tel: (+351) 2 24497

Principal Euro Info Centres

Eurogabinete
Exponur
Leca de Palmeira
P-4450 Matosinhos
Tel: (+351) 29 956940

Eurogabinete
Av Casbal Ribeiro 59
P-1000 Lisbon
Tel: (+351) 1 561071

18
SPAIN

INTRODUCTION

Like most of the European Union countries, Spain has regional dissimilarities, but they are perhaps the most pronounced and wide-ranging of all the countries within the EU. To treat Spain as one country would be a bad mistake. The Catalonians, the Basques, and the Andalusians are quite different people, with different subcultures and business styles.

For instance, a typical Andalusian will be difficult to do business with, unsure of the honesty of his trading partner. He will counter question with question. The Basque and the Andalusian belief in independence will extend to gifts being freely given to ensure that no debt is being incurred by the deal. In Catalonia, however, the people are more European in attitude and outlook. In all cases, the generation gap plays a major role; younger executives are more able to focus on business deals, although contacting the correct person within this group is more important – and more difficult – in order to reduce internal political problems than it is with the older, mainly non-English-speaking generation.

In general, it is true to say that the Spaniards are a proud, even haughty, nation given to perceiving slights where none are intended, but this is balanced by their generosity and sociability, which are difficult to match elsewhere.

MAKING THE APPOINTMENT

It is important to contact the Spanish executive with whom you wish to do business. This should be done in a well-written, formal letter. A telephone call within two weeks of sending the letter is acceptable. However, be sure that the contact is correct; not only is the Spanish business hierarchy very formal (and prepared, in some cases, to accept 'gifts'), there is also considerable jealousy of success. A commitment made by one executive can and might be overturned by his senior if he perceives it as being outside the other's range of business.

Spanish business executives also work very hard at making relationships which are hard to break, regardless of the quality of the new sales proposition. If you suspect that a deal will not progress on its merits, then a telephone call to the Managing Director may break the logjam. This, must be done with great skill so as not to create loss of face for the executive who is subsequently instructed to respond to your initiative.

The role of the secretary is growing. In major companies they play a very European role in handling the executive's diary. The secretary is seen very much as the 'office keeper', to look after the business needs of the executive. If treated in this way, with courtesy, they will be very valuable. However, given the social structure of Spain, they will always remain an 'assistant-to', and will be unlikely to undertake agreements, even to arrange meetings, without further confirmation.

In all communications, especially in open transmission such as telex and facsimile, ensure the sensitivity of the issue is recognised. If you upset a Spanish executive by allowing others to read or react to your requests more effectively than your counterpart is able, it could lead to a deal which might have been done (slowly, perhaps – but done) being stopped. The biggest single problem in doing business is internal politics and envy.

THE MEETING

If you are attending a meeting and are unable to speak Spanish, enquire first of your counterpart if he wishes to discuss business in English, or has someone on his staff who could act as interpreter. Only as the last option offer to bring your own interpreter.

The Spanish, particularly, in Southern Spain, are passionate about their business and express themselves in a great deal of non-verbal behaviour – don't, however, take the lead in this. Back-slapping and hugging is initiated by the Spanish in all but the most intimate and long-standing relationships.

Spanish business meetings can go on for a long time and, if lunch or dinner is offered, even longer. In the small talk surrounding the business propositions the subjects of football and other popular sports are acceptable. However, politics is not. Never join in or show a preference for one side or the other; the Franco days cut deeply into many families.

During the meeting, try to avoid a lecturing approach. The Spanish like to take their time and be seen to be in control of the discussion. To force them to an 'obvious' conclusion will be self-defeating. The greatest emphases will be placed on a good personal relationship and trust. Any contract entered into will be strictly fulfilled, and they will expect no less of you. The passion which is so typically Mediterranean will be used during negotiations and, unless you back them into an impossible position, will be temporary. Haggling is an accepted tactic, and its use is expected. Once an agreement is made, the terms and the spirit will be honoured in the fullest sense, even if personal loss is its consequence. If this is caused by an error by both parties to the deal, the approach must be handled carefully to avoid loss of face.

ENTERTAINING

Business meals

Business lunches take hours, and are usually lavish and alcoholic. The Spanish are used to this, but the large quantities of alcohol may put you at a disadvantage. Lunch begins at about 1.30–2.00 pm with drinks, and can finish around 4.30–5.00 pm. The Spanish will expect you to join and match them in the consumption of drinks; not to do so without an adequate excuse is seen as unfriendly, and medical excuses are the best accepted. Business and non-business topics will be discussed throughout the meal, so you need to remain sharp throughout.

Breakfast meetings are acceptable, but need to be checked out before being offered. Dinner, if taken out, will be between 10.00–11.00 pm.

Being taken to someone's home is a great sign of trust. If you are invited to join your counterpart and his family this is very positive, although it does vary from province to province and is less likely to occur, for example, in Catalonia, where business and pleasure are very separate. For dinner, you are likely to be invited at 8.30 pm for drinks with the meal being served around 9.30 pm. Spanish hospitality and generosity are a way of life. A Spaniard – even if he has little money – will want to pay for the meal regardless of who extends the invitation. It is always polite to offer, but accept that you are unlikely to end up paying.

Subjects for social discussion

It is important to comment upon the family, and children in particular. The Spanish in general enjoy children, and take great pride in their families. If you have a family yourself, this can help. Other areas of discussion are cultural, but remember that there are provincial rivalries so make sure your compliments are appropriate to the region.

Business hospitality

Business hospitality is unusual in Spain, although invitations in the major cultural centres may be offered. In general, the Spanish would expect you to perceive their generous personal hospitality as more important than corporate entertainment.

Gifts

In Spain, it is not the custom to take gifts for the host or hostess when being entertained at a person's home. Never take any. It is acceptable, however, when leaving the country, to send flowers to the lady of the house, thanking her for her hospitality. When you are introduced to the hostess, do not introduce yourself by kissing cheeks. Wait for her to offer hers. Business associates are expected to act according to their perceived cultures, and the British and Dutch are considered to be somewhat distant.

Business gifts, however, are an accepted part of Spanish business life. They are used to cement continuing relationships. Christmas presents in Spain can be very expensive. However, there is a growing backlash against this type of present. Find out the culture within the particular company with which you are dealing: to get it wrong either way could damage both the personal and business relationship.

Dress

A dark-coloured suit and conservative tie are an important part of dress-sense in Spain, although in the provinces a blazer or sports jacket with slacks is acceptable. It is important to look both serious and stylish.

WOMEN IN BUSINESS

Women are not expected to (and therefore usually do not) reach senior levels of management. Men, although polite, are unlikely to treat a woman with the same peer-level respect as a male counterpart would command. Business with a woman may well take longer and be culturally more difficult for a Spaniard (particularly of the older generation) to deal with.

WORKING HOURS AND PUBLIC HOLIDAYS

The day is divided into two. An 8.30 or 9.00 am start is usual
with work continuing until 1.00 pm. Lunch, particularly in the
provinces, is usually taken at home and never in the office
which closes until 4.30 pm. Work then recommences until about
7.30–8.30 pm. In summertime, this changes and the offices are
only open from 7.30 am until 2.30 pm. This is called *journada
intensive*. Those offices which need to remain open will only
have a skeleton staff.

Public holidays are:

1st January	(New Year's Day)
6th January	(Epiphany)
19th March	(St Joseph's Day)
1st May	(Labour Day)
25th July	(St James's Day)
15th August	(Assumption)
12th October	(Columbus' Day)
1st November	(All Saints' Day)
8th December	(Immaculate Conception)
25th December	(Christmas Day)

In addition, there are three movable days, including Good
Friday and Easter Monday.

LETTER-WRITING

The envelope

Spanish	English
Sr D (initials, surnames)	Mr
Sra Doña (initials, surnames)	Mrs
Srta (initials, surnames)	Miss

Salutation

Spanish	Letter written in: English
Muy Sr mío	Dear Mr (first surname)
	Dear Sr (first surname)
Muy Sra mía	Dear Mrs (first surname)
	Dear Sra (first surname)

Srta (first surname)   Dear Miss (first surname)
                                  Dear Srta (first surname)
Muy Sr mío, Muy Sra mía   Dear Sir, Madam
Muy Srs míos   Dear Sirs

Closing
Individual   Le saluda atentamente   Yours sincerely
Company   Le saluda atentamente   Yours faithfully

Note

If the letter is written in Spanish, the surname is omitted in the salutation.

MARKETING

Advertising expenditure has grown by 25 per cent per annum since 1984. This increase in expenditure has benefited all segments of the media alike, with media owners launching competitive media to provide a full range of services. Research facilities to match the greater range of media opportunities are also rapidly being developed in a country whose 40 million inhabitants are seen as a core attraction by many EC countries.

The consumer base has five classifications and is broken down as follows:

Table 18.1   Consumer classifications in Spain

	%
Upper	7.0
Upper Middle	20.0
Middle	32.0
Lower Middle	18.0
Lower	23.0

Source INE

Media

All advertising in Spain, except in the Canary Islands, is subject to VAT (known as TVA) at 12 per cent. Television advertising of alcoholic drinks, tobacco and prescription drugs is prohibited in all parts of Spain. Advertisements for financial and pharmaceutical products require administrative authorisation.

Spending is split in the media as follows:

Table 18.2   Media spend in Spain

	%
Newspapers	33.0
Magazines	17.0
Television	32.0
Radio	13.0
Cinema	0.5
Outdoor	4.5

Source JWT, Madrid

The spend rankings by key categories are:

Table 18.3   Key categories spend in Spain

(1) Food
(2) Transport (including cars)
(3) Alcoholic and non-
    alcoholic drinks
(4) Beauty and hygiene
(5) Services, public
    and private
(6) Finance, insurance
(7) Commerce
(8) Household goods
(9) Tobacco

Source Repress (Nielsen)

CONSUMER PREFERENCES/DIFFERENCES

Household spend

The Spanish desire a beautiful home above most things and
this is reflected on the amount they spend on the furnishings
for their home. Because they have a strong home market,
however, furnishings that are bought tend to be made in Spain.
This does not indicate a bias in the Spanish purchasing trend
but merely indicates price and market availability.

Market penetration of household goods is quite poor
considering the regional wealth differences. An example of
this reflection is in the number of stoves bought *per capita*,

which is less than the number, again *per capita*, bought in Portugal. However, consumer spend penetration is growing.

The breakdown of the household spend on goods and services is found below.

Financial awareness

The Spanish are one of the lowest banked countries in the EU with only 34 per cent of the population having bank accounts. There is also a low usage of other financial products at all levels. However, market penetration of credit cards is as high as in the UK.

The lack of use of different savings and investments is reflected by the spend priority given by the Spanish; research indicates that they would select as a priority holidays, cars or a second home.

Table 18.4   Household spend in Spain

Items	%
Furniture (including carpets and other floor coverings)	37
White goods	13
Furnishings	8
Table utensils	14
Domestic and other household services	28

Source Eurostat/Mintel

Food spend

The Spanish consume more meat *per capita* than the British although over the last ten years this trend has slowed down. Pork and poultry are the preferred choices.

Despite being a sizeable wine producing nation, the Spanish preference is for beer which is drunk more than wine. Interestingly, Spanish consumers have one of the highest levels of desire in wanting a wider choice of alcohol-free drinks. This also reflects the consumers' desire to increase the availability of additive-free and low fat foods.

General consumer spend

The Spanish desire for clothes is low on the priority spend scale, indeed, the Spanish spend is almost the same as the Greeks and Portuguese.

Political trends

The Spanish have six political parties to consider when casting their Euro vote. Out of a total of 60 Euro seats, the Socialists still held on to power retaining 27 out of the 28 at the last Euro election.

The percentage of voter turnout in Spain is 55 per cent, just below the EU average of 59 per cent.

Green issues in Spain did not attract as much voter awareness as, say, in Italy.

ESTABLISHING A BUSINESS

Authorisation for investments by private investors from abroad are generally not required. However, the investment does require prior verification as a control measure by the Department of Foreign Transactions (DGTE) for the following types of investment:

1. The acquisition of more than 50 per cent of the capital of a Spanish company.
2. The formation of branches or establishments.
3. In certain cases, the acquisition of real property by foreign individuals not resident in Spain, and the acquisition of real property by a legal entity.

Special rules apply to certain sectors of the economy, for example telecommunications, banking, defence and air transport.

The most common ways for a foreign investor to operate in Spain are through a joint venture, a branch or a subsidiary company. A minimum of three shareholders (acting on their own behalf or on the behalf of other companies or individuals) are required to form an SA company (*Sociedad Anonima*). There is no minimum or maximum capital requirement to form an SA company and ownership can be by a variety of shares.

For a *Sociedad de Responsabilidad Limitada* (SRL), the capital is divided into participations which are equal in value and are indivisible. The number of members cannot exceed 50 and the maximum capitalisation of an SRL is Pts 50,000,000.

Management structure

In an SRL, the company is represented by an administrator who need not be a shareholder, and the company may only have one administrator. No auditors are required for an SRL.

In an SA, the company is governed by a Board of Directors, or by a sole director. If there is a board, then three directors are required. As with an SRL, no auditors are required by law unless the company is listed on the Stock Exchange, or is a bank. However, the articles can require the appointment of auditors. Currently, there are no employee participation requirements.

USEFUL ADDRESSES

Sources of information and help

Spanish Chamber of Commerce
5 Cavendish Square
London W1M 0DP
Tel: 071-637 9061
Fax: 071-436 7188

British Chamber of Commerce in Spain
Calle Marques de Valdeiglesias 3
E-28004
Madrid 4
Tel: (+34) 1 521 9622
Tlx: 45522 COBE E

Research sources

Instituto Dym SA (subsidiary of AGB Research)
Corcega 329 4a
E-08037 Barcelona
Tel: (+34) 3 2374480
Tlx: 50872 DYM E

Addresses for advertisers

Spanish Association of Advertising Agencies
10–59 Velazques
Madrid
Tel: (+34) 1 435 6983

Chambers of Commerce

Barcelona   Ample 11
                  Barcelona
                  Tel: (+34) 3 302 3366

Bilbao	Robriquez Arias 6
	Bilbao
	Tel: (+34) 4 423 8546
Madrid	Plaza de la Independencia 1
	Madrid
	Tel: (+34) 42 7193

Principal Euro Info Centres

Centro Europeo de Informacion
Av Diagonal 403 ir
E-08008 Barcelona
Tel: (+34) 3217 20 08

Centro Europeo de Informacion
Alamdea de Recaldo 50
E-48008 Bilbao (Vizcaya)
Tel: (+34)4 4444 054

Centro Europeo de Informacion
Diego de Leon 50
E-28006 Madrid
Tel: (+34) 1262 44 10

Centro Europeo de Informacion
Avda San Fransisco Javier s/n
Edificio Sevilla 2-9a Planta
E-41005 Seville
Tel: (+34) 54 65 04 11

19
THE UNITED KINGDOM

INTRODUCTION

The business culture within Britain is rapidly evolving from the days of rigid social and educational hierarchies to one of a more entrepreneurial environment. This process has been championed by Thatcherite policies and initiatives. It would be wrong, however, particularly in the City of London, to assume that ability, drive and ambition have yet overtaken the traditional social advantages of belonging to the 'right family' (old money), having a public school education (fee paying), and going to the right university, namely Oxford or Cambridge.

The UK is socially and economically split between the Midlands, the North, Scotland, Northern Ireland and Wales (collectively called The North if you speak to a Southerner) where the country's light and heavy engineering industries exist, and the generally more affluent South, where service industries predominate. A line drawn on a map from Bristol to Norwich would approximate this imaginary divide.

In all business transactions with Britons, punctuality, initial formality, politeness, sincerity and a good grasp of the English language are essential.

MAKING THE APPOINTMENT

British business still retains quite rigid, self-important power hierarchies. Many British managers will not admit to their limitations in the decision-making process and, although often speaking with convincing authority, they may have little real influence over the business decision. The most effective way of ascertaining the right person to contact is by writing direct to the owner of a small company, or to the 'Chief Executive', 'Managing Director' or 'Chairman' of a large company. In some companies, one person will hold two or three of these titles, so a telephone call to his secretary would identify his preferred form of address.

The decision-making body within medium or large British companies is normally the company's Board of Directors. Membership of this Board will be sought by most ambitious managers, and carries the title 'Director'. In most companies, the function of the individual director will precede the title, eg 'Sales Director', 'Operations Director', 'Finance Director', etc. Directors always outrank managers, with the exception of a General Manager, who will run a whole division, factory or major store for a company, and who will usually have directors reporting to him.

Differences in status are highlighted on business cards, which are generally offered more frequently the lower the status of the contact. This does not apply to guests offering their own cards; however, cards are used less frequently now than in the past.

The formality of British business would support initial contact through a well-written, appropriately addressed, well-researched letter. Men should be addressed as 'Mr' unless they have a title such as 'Sir', or 'Lord'. Women should be addressed as 'Mrs' if married, 'Miss' if single and 'Ms' if their marital status is unknown or if this is the preferred form of address. It is always better to address your letter to a named person within an organisation, and it should conclude 'Yours sincerely', with your own name and position underneath your signature. If you are really unable to find out the name of the person you wish to contact and do not know the sex of that person, never begin a letter 'Dear Sir or Madam'. Use 'Dear Sir' and conclude with 'Yours faithfully'.

Once you are on first name terms with your contact, it is perfectly acceptable to open a letter with 'Dear John', but note that it would be taken as a withdrawal of friendship to revert to surnames once first names have been used.

Following up the letter with a telephone call after an appropriate time is acceptable, and it is always a good idea to make friends with your contact's secretary. Time spent in building up a relationship with the latter will assist in getting your name into the decision-maker's diary (often controlled by the secretary). Do not assume that being offered an appointment with someone other than the initial contact is a slight. Interest has been shown and the correct communication channels defined for you.

Where it is likely that your business is unknown to the target company, it is useful to send corporate information beforehand, although do not be surprised if you get the impression that it has been read immediately prior to your meeting. This is, indeed, quite possible; the British are not famed for their preparation.

THE MEETING

It is unlikely that anyone other than those needed to discuss the proposal will be invited to the meeting by the British host, and he will almost certainly hold the meeting in his own offices. The discussion will usually begin and close with social conversation and the business discussion will be conducted with great politeness. However, it would be most unusual for minutes to be taken and a brief letter from you summarising the discussion is often advisable. This will serve to confirm any action you are about to take as a result of your discussions and can help to avoid decisions being reversed after the meeting. Some British managers are, unfortunately, apt to change their minds and be far less decisive after the meeting than during it.

The timing of the initial or subsequent appointments will indicate the appropriateness of entertainment.

ENTERTAINING

Business meals

Although the most ambitious British manager will start work at around 8.00–8.30 am (earlier if his factory is open) and finish around 6.30–7.00 pm, he has not yet quite taken to breakfast meetings. These are appropriate if taken en route to another meeting (say, on a train) or if you are staying at the same hotel overnight.

If a meeting is arranged close to noon, a lunch invitation will be given. If it is not forthcoming at the first meeting, however, this is not a negative indication. Either party can offer lunch, but the visitor should give the host ample time to suggest it. Business lunches are at least 50 per cent social, and serious business is often left until the coffee is served. It would be unusual for papers to be exchanged or referred to at the luncheon table. Aperitifs and wine are usual with the meal, which will normally take upwards of 90 minutes. If the invitation to lunch is yours, the British host can be offered the choice of restaurant, or you may choose it yourself. It is generally safest to stick to English or French cuisine, but, if you are planning something more exotic, check with your host's secretary whether he is likely to enjoy your choice.

The person offering the invitation usually pays the bill, although some British managers may insist on paying. It is wise to give in gracefully, after a short debate.

Business dinners are offered less frequently than lunches, and tend to be more friendly affairs. The same rules apply as to lunch, although business is even less likely to be discussed openly. The issue can be introduced, but should be dropped if the host seems unenthusiastic.

British businesspeople tend to leave work between 5.00 and 6.00 pm, and take large amounts of work home with them. However, this desire to be home does not mean that an invitation to drinks after normal office hours will not be accepted. They are generally prepared to take business telephone calls out of hours once they offer their home number, but these should always be made in the early evening, and not later than 9.30 pm. Most business people will be unavailable during their two- or three-week family summer holiday, usually taken during the school vacation from late July to early September.

The British are prepared more than most to offer invitations to their homes. Although the acceptance to these is not a must, they do indicate a desire to build a positive relationship, and should be accepted if possible. It is appropriate to take a small gift of flowers, wine or chocolates, and a short note of thanks should be sent the following day.

Subjects for social discussion

Yes	No
Children	Politics
Headline news	War
Climate	Religion
Problems with the journey	Education
Sport	
Cars, houses and estates	

Business hospitality

Away from the business stage, business entertaining (designed to develop personal as well as business advantage) is common in Britain. The events offered vary greatly and may cover occasions where the host is the sponsor of the event to those which have particular importance to the British. These fall into two categories: the first being events where scarcity of tickets indicates the standing of the host company (eg Centre Court tickets for Wimbledon, Wembley Cup Final, etc), and second events at which it is socially advantageous to be seen (eg Ascot, Henley and Glyndebourne). Declining an invitation (backed, of course, by the appropriate excuses) is unlikely to cause major offence but business opportunities beyond the immediate may be lost, since such events often provide a wealth of contacts for the future.

It is unlikely that you will be in any way compromised by accepting such invitations and, even when a dinner invitation turns into a trip to a night-club, the British sense of propriety is generally evident.

Invitations may be offered to you alone, but where cultural evening events are proposed then the invitation will almost invariably include your spouse or partner.

The visitor is not expected to reciprocate, but a return invitation will usually be accepted. Care needs to be taken, though, to ensure that good faith is not lost. For instance, it is not wise to invite a more senior member of the organisation than you are dealing with instead of your contact, but it is good form to let him know of the invitation and gain his implicit acceptance.

Gifts

Business gifts are a part of business life between supplier and retailer, buyer and seller. In fact, around Christmas time business gifts are as expected as Christmas cards. The value of such gifts varies enormously, but is usually calculated so that it neither offends nor could be construed as a bribe.

Dress

In all business meetings it is best to dress in a fairly traditional manner. This means dark-coloured lounge suits for men (black, dark blue or grey), plain or striped shirts, good quality ties in non-garish colours and polished black shoes. For women, more colour can be introduced, but dress should not be flamboyant. A man is still judged by his appearance: brown shoes, nylon shirts or matching tie, shirt and handkerchief can definitely create the 'wrong' initial impression.

Invitations to cocktail parties or more formal occasions will usually indicate dress requirements: for example, 'black tie' (dinner jacket and black bow tie) and long dresses for ladies, or 'lounge suits' and 'cocktail dresses' for less formal affairs.

WOMEN IN BUSINESS

Few women outside the service industries hold senior jobs. Attitudes to women tend to vary with a man's age and past experience. Prejudice, where it exists, usually takes the form of condescension.

WORKING HOURS AND PUBLIC HOLIDAYS

The average working week is from 9.00 am to 5.30 pm, Monday to Friday. In industry, these hours may vary, often starting and finishing earlier than offices.

On average, Britons have four weeks' annual holiday. They will usually take two to three weeks in the summer, plus some extra time around Christmas. There is an increasing trend of taking winter sports holidays.

Public holidays are:

1st January	(New Year's Day)
	(Scotland one day longer)
1st Monday in May	(May Day)
Last Monday in May	(Spring Bank Holiday)
Last Monday in August	(August Bank Holiday)
25th December	(Christmas Day)
26th December	(Boxing Day)

In addition, there are two movable days, Good Friday and Easter Monday.

LETTER-WRITING

The envelope

To a man:	Mr (initials, surname), or (initials, surname) Esq[a]
To a married woman:	Mrs (initials, surname), or Ms[b] (initials, surname)
To an unmarried woman:	Miss (initials, surname), or Ms[b] (initials, surname)

Salutation

To a man:	Dear Mr (surname)
To a married woman:	Dear Mrs/Ms (surname)
To an unmarried woman:	Dear Miss/Ms (surname)
To an unnamed person:	Dear Sir, Madam
To a company:	Dear Sirs
Closing	
To a named individual:	Yours sincerely
To an unnamed individual or company	Yours faithfully

Notes
[a] Formerly used as a mark of respect, particularly for proprietors of companies. Now rarely used.
[b] The title 'Ms' can be used where the woman's marital status is unknown, or where this is the preferred form of address. It is widely used by women in business.

MARKETING

The British economy has experienced a massive change in direction and focus since 1979. The introduction of free-market practices backed by monetarist economic policies and a *laissez-faire* political attitude have altered many of the country's business practices. However, advertising spending is still seen by business as a potential short-term route to protect the 'bottom line'.

The classification of consumers purchasing trends for marketing purposes into identifiable sectors has formed the cornerstone of most promotional strategies. The most common and basic classification is 'socio-economic grading'. Within the system there are five socio-economic grades:

Table 19.1   Socio-economic grading in the UK

Social grade	Percentage of population	Social status	Head of household's occupation
A	3	Upper middle class	Higher managerial, administrative or professional
B	10	Middle class	Intermediate managerial,

Social grade	Percentage of population	Social status	Head of household's occupation
			administrative or professional
C	24	Lower middle class	Supervisory or clerical, and junior managerial administrative or professional
C_2	30	Skilled working class	Skilled manual workers
D	25	Working class	Semi-skilled and unskilled manual workers
E	8	Lowest levels of subsistence	State pensioners or widows (no other earner) casual or lowest grade worker

Source JICNARS (Joint Industry Committee for National Readership Surveys)

More sophisticated life-style classifications are available, based on attributes other than occupation which give more meaningful and usable data. The initial classification of this type was developed by CACI Market Analysis and is called ACORN.

The split in the advertising pound in the media is approximately as follows:

Table 19.2   Media spend in the UK

	%
Press	61
TV	32
Poster and transport	4
Cinema	1
Radio	2

Source MEAL (Media Expenditure Analysis Ltd)

Media

VAT at 17.5 per cent is payable on all production and media costs for TV, outdoor, cinema and radio advertising. A levy of 0.1 per cent of gross media costs for press (except classified lineage and semi-display), outdoor, cinema and direct mail is applied to fund the Advertising Standards Authority (ASA). A special code of practice for sales promotion is in operation under the supervision of the ASA. No advertising for cigarettes is allowed on TV, nor in cinemas showing children's programmes. Spirits advertising is not banned on TV by the government, but Independent Television (ITV) companies do not accept spirits advertising: this is in keeping with their voluntary control system. Alcoholic drinks advertising may not be shown within, or around, programmes for children, or between 4.00 and 6.00 pm on weekdays. There are many restrictions for other advertising on TV, radio and in the press. For more information contact: The Independent Broadcasting Authority (IBA), 70 Brompton Road, London SW3 1EY (Tel: 071-584 7011); and Advertising Standards Authority, Brook House, Torrington Place, London WC1E 7HN (Tel: 071-580 5555).

The UK national daily press is divided between the serious press which covers business, and the popular press which does not (at least not seriously). The key papers for business are the *Financial Times*, followed by *The Times*, *Daily Telegraph*, *Independent* and *Guardian*. Sunday papers which cover business are the *Observer*, *Sunday Telegraph* and *Sunday Times*. There are a number of magazines which are published weekly and monthly: *The Economist*, *Investor's Chronicle* and *Financial Weekly* appear weekly and *Management Today* appears monthly.

The spend rankings by key categories are:

Table 19.3   Key categories in spending in the UK

		£m
(1)	Food	5.1
(2)	Retail, mail order	4.1
(3)	Financial	3.5
(4)	Automotive	3.2
(5)	Drink	2.0
(6)	Household stores	1.8
(7)	Toiletries, cosmetics	1.7
(8)	Leisure equipment	1.5
(9)	Holidays, transport	1.4
(10)	Household appliances	1.1

Source MEAL

CONSUMER PREFERENCES/DIFFERENCES

Household spend

The British have the highest ownership in the EU of leisure electrical appliances, this can be seen in the volume of purchase in videos and homecomputers which ranks the highest in EU, and on purchase of stereo equipment which ranks second to Germany. Indeed, despite the present Government's desire to see these imported goods reduced, the consumer spend on these items is still continuing.

In the overall spend on home furnishings, the British, like the Spanish, are middle-ranking spenders but when compared to Northern EU countries Britain is at the bottom of the furnishings league spend table. Interestingly, the spend on white goods is high.

The breakdown of the household spend on goods and services is as follows.

Table 19.4   Household spend in the UK

Items	%
Furniture (including carpets and other floor coverings)	29
White goods	25
Furnishings	9
Table utensils	13
Domestic and other household services	24

Source Eurostat/Mintel

Financial awareness

With Britain currently seen as the financial centre of Europe, it is not surprising to learn that the British are well banked, with a greater percentage of the population holding both a building society and a personal bank account. But if a central bank of Europe should be located in Germany then this will no doubt affect the volume of business in the future.

Britain (like France and Germany) tends to follow consumer trend patterns from the US, as can be seen in the penetration of credit cards which is one of the highest in the EU.

Food spend

Only the Germans and the Belgians drink more beer than the British. In other liquid consumption there has been a marked increase in the purchase of both mineral water and wine. The British, without doubt, drink more tea (both bagged and loose) than any other country in the Community.

Food spend levels on biscuits and chocolate are the highest in the EU, with many international companies trying to win their share of the confectionary market in the UK.

More milk is consumed in Britain than elsewhere and sales of other dairy products are high. Health awareness is growing and this is shown in a reduction in the consumption of food with a high fat content. British cheese is having a revival, especially farm-produced, although cheese import from EU countries is high.

Interestingly, in Britain the consumption of meat, poultry and fish differs from region to region with the West Midlands consuming more meat than the South East or North West.

Over the last decade, the British have become more used to eating out or buying take-away foods.

Hypermarkets and supermarkets are widely used although a recent trend shows that consumers desire a return to the 'high street' type of shop with its old fashioned, sometimes Victorian, appearance.

General consumer trends

Britain ranks third in the purchase of passenger cars although unlike France and Italy, there is no home-brand loyalty.

The British are gradually becoming more aware of green issues with recent surveys showing that the consumer will pay more for environmentally-friendly products. The British car industry, however, has yet to match the environmentally-friendly Germans.

Political trends

Environmental issues played an important role for the first time in the British electorate's opinion. Although the Green Party had over 2 million votes cast, no UK Green MEPs hold a seat as Britain still has not adopted proportional representation.

Britain is the bottom of the league table in voter turnout showing a mere 36 per cent.

Out of 81 Euro seats, the Labour Party gained 13 seats more than the Conservative Party (Labour 45, Conservative 32).

ESTABLISHING A BUSINESS

No permission is required to establish a business presence in the UK and there are no exchange controls. A foreign corporation may establish either a subsidiary or a branch in the United Kingdom. Most foreign companies set up a local private company (Ltd) rather than a public company (Plc). No consents are needed; no local shareholders or directors are required; minimum capital of £100 issued shares apply to companies. Capital duty (1 per cent) is due on shares issued; certain documents (for example, memorandum and articles of association) have to be filed. A foreign corporation which sets up a UK branch must, within 30 days, register certain documents (with an English translation) and appoint a local representative.

Management structure

In the UK, the features of public and private companies are not as distinct as they are in other European countries. There are no minimum capital requirements for the registration of a private company, and shares can be issued in different classes. The company acts through directors, and those whom they appoint to run the company.

A private company must have at least one director, who can be the shareholder, and a company secretary. The company secretary acts as the chief administrative officer. Non-executive directors are not employed by the company and have no individual power as directors to bind the company in business, other than as a member of the board.

In public limited companies (plc), the company will usually have, in addition to its main board, a management committee. The main board will consist of both executive and non-executive directors, who will usually be appointed by the Chairman. The link between management and board is the Managing Director or Chief Executive. A Company Secretary in a public company must have the relevant company secretarial qualifications. Otherwise, apart from a minimum authorised capital of £50,000, the structure is the same as for a private company, or 'close' company (five directors or less).

Audited accounts must be filed each year with Companies House based in Cardiff. In addition, accounts have to be filed with the Inland Revenue. Sole traders or partnerships need only file accounts with the Inland Revenue.

There are no formal worker participation requirements for UK companies, and no legal requirements for worker councils, although relationships with trades unions are emerging from a phase of economic co-operation.

Businesses can also be conducted through a partnership or

as a sole trader, in which case the income is taxed in the hands of the individual or the partners, whichever is applicable.

USEFUL ADDRESSES

Sources of information and help

Association of British Chambers of Commerce
4 Westwood House
Westwood Business Park
Coventry CV4 8HS
Tel: 0203 694484

Research sources

A. C. Nielsen (all Nielsen's European operations are
    co-ordinated from this office)
Nielsen House
London Road
Headington
Oxford OX3 9RX
Tel: 0865 742742
Tlx: 83136

Market Research Society
15 Northburgh Street
London EC1V 0AH
Tel: 071 490 4911

Addresses for advertisers

Advertising Standards Authority
Brook House
Torrington Place
London WC1E 7HN
Tel: 071 580 5555
Fax: 071 631 3051

Independent Broadcasting Authority
70 Brompton Road
London SW3 1EY
Tel: 071 584 7011

Institute of Marketing
Moor Hall
Cookham
Berks SL6 9QH
Tel: 0628 524922
Fax: 0628 531382

Institute of Practitioners in Advertising
44 Belgrave Square
London SW1 8QS
Tel: 071 235 7020

Chambers of Commerce

Aberdeen	5 Hadden Street Aberdeen AB9 1HS Tel: 0224 212626 Fax: 0224 213221
Belfast	22 Great Victoria Street Belfast BT2 7BJ Tel: 0232 244113 Fax: 0232 247024
Birmingham	PO Box 360 75 Harborne Road Birmingham B15 3DH Tel: 021 454 6171 Fax: 021 455 8670
Bristol	16 Clifton Park Bristol BS8 3BY Tel: 0272 467081 Fax: 0272 238024
Cardiff	101–108 The Exchange Mount Stuart Square Cardiff CF1 6RD Tel: 0222 481648 Fax: 0222 489785
Edinburgh	3 Randolph Crescent Edinburgh EH3 7UD Tel: 031 225 5851 Fax: 031 220 1508

Glasgow	30 George Square
	Glasgow G2 1EQ
	Tel: 041 204 2121
	Fax: 041 221 2336
Leeds	Commerce House
	2 St Albans Place
	Wade Lane
	Leeds LS2 8HZ
	Tel: 0532 430491
	Fax: 0532 430504
London	33 Queen Street
	London EC4R 1AP
	Tel: 071 248 4444
Manchester	56 Oxford Street
	Manchester M60 7HJ
	Tel: 061 236 3210
	Fax: 061 236 4160
Tyne and Wear	65 Quayside
	Newcastle upon Tyne NE1 3DS
	Tel: 091 230 3319
	Fax: 091 261 4035

Principle Euro Info Centres

Euro Info Centre
8 Storey's Gate
London SW1P 3AT
Tel: 071 973 1992

Euro Info Centre
4 Cathedral Road
Cardiff CF1 9JG
Tel: 0222 371631

Euro Info Centre
Windsor House
9–15 Bedford Street
Belfast BT2 7EG
Tel: 0232 240708

Euro Info Centre
7 Alva Street
Edinburgh EH2 4PH
Tel: 031 225 2058

INDEX